Katholikos

The Supernatural

A Rational View of the Divine Word and of the Dual Nature of Man

Katholikos

The Supernatural
A Rational View of the Divine Word and of the Dual Nature of Man

ISBN/EAN: 9783337778361

Printed in Europe, USA, Canada, Australia, Japan

Cover: Foto ©Lupo / pixelio.de

More available books at **www.hansebooks.com**

THE SUPERNATURAL.

A Rational View of the Divine Word,

AND OF

The Dual Nature of Man.

BY
KATHOLIKOS.

WITH INTRODUCTION
BY THE
REV. J. W. REYNOLDS, M.A.,
PREBENDARY OF ST. PAUL'S.

BOSTON:
LEE AND SHEPARD, PUBLISHERS.
1897.

THIS HUMBLE ATTEMPT
TO BRING TRUTH HOME TO THE HEARTS OF
INDIVIDUAL MEMBERS OF THE GREAT HUMAN FAMILY

Is Dedicated

TO THE SONS AND DAUGHTERS OF GOD'S CHURCH IN ENGLAND

IN LOVING MEMORY OF

A FAITHFUL SOLDIER OF THE CROSS.

PREFACE.

THE writer of this work is fully aware that the grave subject which is presented to the consideration of the reader might have been better handled by a deeper thinker; but the book may lead some to study a matter which is often regarded as not in harmony with the intellectual development of the age. It treats of a subject which is of the very highest importance to men, on account of its direct influence upon character. The object of the author is to bring before the rising generation, in as simple a form as possible, the fact, which scientific writers are proving by each new discovery they make, that there is not a single thing in creation, great or small, which does not, when rightly understood, show, *per se*, that it was made by One who had all power, all knowledge, and all skill; and that this Maker is *now*, as in the moment of creation, unchanged in His designs and purposes. The same laws govern the universe to-day as governed it countless ages ago. The logical consequence of this fact is too often ignored, even if it is not openly denied.

When St. Paul said, as he stood on Mars' Hill, 'Ye men of Athens, in all things I perceive that ye are somewhat superstitious, for as I passed along and observed the objects of your worship, I found also an altar with this inscription, To the unknown God: what therefore ye worship in ignorance, this set I forth unto you,' he was but doing what creation is doing continuously; and scientific men unintentionally endorse the proclamation by every new fact which they discover and unfold.

It may be that as their love towards the Author of their being has grown cold, He has withdrawn from them for a time, and left them to substitute Nature for Nature's God, if, as free agents, they choose so to do; but it will not be always so. The Father of mankind is from everlasting to everlasting, and He has said, 'For a small moment have I forsaken thee; but with great mercies will I gather thee. In a little wrath I hid My face from thee for a moment; but with everlasting kindness I will have mercy on thee.' Meanwhile, the men who are working in spiritual darkness for a time, with only the light kindled by themselves as their guide, are doing a great work by unveiling the hidden wonders of creation; for each disclosure is a fresh proof of the wisdom and almightiness of the eternal, unchanging God.

PREFACE

Two Bishops of the Church of England have recently made the statement that 'the great want of the age is a belief in the Supernatural.' That it is so all thoughtful members of the Catholic and Apostolic Church have long been convinced. To help others to attain to a clearer knowledge of themselves, and in so doing to grasp the full meaning of eternity and immortality, and the bearing these must have, when duly realized, upon the life of man in time, is an object worth aiming at, however short of the mark the arrow may fall.

Should the atheist or the sceptic condescend to open this book, the writer ventures to ask him to take a really practical and unprejudiced view of its subject; and in order that he may do so, to place himself in the only logically fair position. That position may be defined (1) negatively. No bias of the mental nature must be allowed to have any weight. No opinions of other men, whose theories may have come under consideration, should be allowed to have more influence over the mind than evidence in a court of justice has on the minds of the jurors until they have heard the counter-evidence. And there must be no 'begging the question,' for that is the coward's part. The brave man will look friend or foe in the face, say what he thinks, do what he believes to be right, and take the consequences, whatever they may be. The really brave and true man can afford to be beaten, and to acknowledge that he is vanquished; because true manliness tells him that no one can do more than his best, and having done that, if failure come it is not the result of his having left undone what he ought to have done; whereas the coward who shuffles and evades questions, even if he succeed in achieving anything, is never sure of the ground on which he is standing; and, if he fail, would rather tell a lie than admit having failed through any fault of his own. (2) The position that a brave, honest man who is seeking truth must take may be defined, affirmatively, in a few words—he must confront Christ. As a son of Adam, and a lord of creation, let him take the place of judge, and try Christ, not after the fashion of Herod, or of Pilate, but as a just and honest judge would try a person who was accused by an avowed enemy of a crime of which the life of the accused, so far as it was known, rendered it impossible to believe him guilty. The case would then stand thus—Jesus, the Son of Mary, a daughter of the house of David, claimed to be the only begotten Son of God, the Maker of all things, visible and invisible; equal to the Father as touching His Godhead, and inferior to the Father as touching His manhood. He claimed to be the second Person of the co-equal and co-eternal Trinity. He claimed to be the Messiah of whom the prophets wrote; the Redeemer of fallen man; the Royal Child who was to be born at Bethlehem; who was to be called 'Wonderful Counsellor, the Mighty God, the everlasting Father, the Prince of Peace,' and of whose kingdom there was to be no end. Now Christ *was* all this, higher, mightier, and holier than the mind can conceive or words can tell, or He was—what? One dare not put into words what He, in whom His judges, accusers, and murderers could find no fault at all, *must be*, if He were *not* God Incarnate, the Saviour of the world.

Let all honest doubters face the question—What WAS the Man who went about doing only good, if He was not the Christ of God? And then let them try to prove that the sacred books of the Jews are modern forgeries like the Isidore Decretals of the Papacy; that the life of Jesus of Nazareth is but an interesting fiction. And let them try to give adequate reasons—that will satisfy themselves and others—for *believing* the history of the landing of Cæsar in the British Isles, and the occupation of those isles by the Romans; and for *disbelieving* the Life, Resurrection, and Ascension of Jesus Christ. The result would be a glorious triumph; for out of the darkness would shine a bright light, and in that light they would surely find the Author of Light.

CONTENTS.

CHAPTER	PAGE
INTRODUCTION	xiii
I. THE REALITY OF THE SUPERNATURAL	1
II. THE GREAT SACRAMENT—GOD IN NATURE	46
III. THE GREAT PROCESSION	111
IV. THE GREAT KINGDOM	175

INTRODUCTION.

BY

JOSEPH WILLIAM REYNOLDS, M.A.,

PREBENDARY OF ST. PAUL'S;

Author of 'The Supernatural in Nature, a Verification by Free Use of Science,' 'The World to Come. Immortality a Physical Fact,' etc.

THIS book is remarkable for historical illustrations, felicity of expression, correct reasoning, and truthful zeal. It is not a laborious, argumentative treatise on a difficult subject; but an intelligent, well-reasoned explanation, pleasant and easy. A large class of readers will find it not less interesting than useful. Every thoughtful, honest reader will derive benefit from the perusal. The four chapters are as Gospels of the Supernatural.

REALITY OF THE SUPERNATURAL.

The writer bravely, and with not less skill, confronts the spirit of the age with just censure, for being in doubt as to that very thing which renders existence very beautiful, and of surpassing wonder.

The realities revealed by Scripture, and of which Creation is the natural veil, are those supreme verities which awake our interest, while in the body, as to future experience when out of the body. Life, which gathers the particles of which our frame is composed, has an inner light—the soul; and a spirit, with kindling from above, that gives a yet higher essence. This higher essence not only aggrandizes our mortality, but conveys everlastingness. It renews body and soul at the resurrection into the likeness of Christ in Glory. Events like the Conversion of St. Paul are as stars in earth's sky, smiling streamlets from the higher splendour.

Abuse of knowledge so thickens and darkens the material veil that, to the natural eye, God is hidden, not revealed in Creation. Advanced science comes to our help, and reveals that Death is not a nothingness, nor an empty space whither life after life, and world after world, are carried and made desolate; but peopled with many sweet influences. These influences, during the intermediate state, are the seal set upon our completion. Whatever good exists now will reappear sometime, somewhere; nothing is lost.

Present attainments are, as by a mountainous ascent, achieved with cost and pain. Summits attained are but steps to higher ascents. Sometimes mental weakness, evil appetites, make us grovel. The superstitions and prejudices of a self-satisfied unbelief, arising from the narrowness of merely physical investigation, incapacitate not a few for full completion, and achievement of life's great honours. They lose the glory of a knowledge that conquers. The great should emulate grand old Abraham's faith. The lowly are to be pure and devout, that even if taken from the rich man's gate, they may dwell where are many angels.

We cannot rid ourselves of the Supernatural. The standard within every man of right and wrong is an impress from One who will judge. Our hope and fear show that there is more than to-day, more than to-morrow, to be cared for; a future demands and enforces consideration. In vain do a few individuals, dreading that future, endeavour to stifle the thought and feeling that remind them of it. The difficulty and danger, the few cases in which subterfuges are an anodyne, make certain the unnaturalness, and failure, of trying to live without regard to the Supernatural. We cannot help believing in the unseen. It is that from which Nature came. It is that to which Nature will return. It is that wherein we shall be perfected.

Every thing, every force, is conserved: there is an after-state for all. The nature of that hereafter will be in analogy with that of which the present is capable. The individuality of every kind of life, or personality, is possessed even by the dead; molecular motions are various as the differences of structure; and these naturally influence future conditions. If there were no future state, we could not think of it at all. Our thoughts of that state arise from our noblest, and therefore our truest faculties.

The Great Sacrament: God in Nature.

The unity of matter and force in life and sensation, in the mental and moral, are a sacramental mystery. The different elements, most different, are made into the structure—man. He is an epitome of the universe. Divine power, life, thought, are writ small in him.

He, a living temple, is naturally furnished with a sense of the Supernatural. This sense often rises into a felt fulness of the All Great. When in darkness he yet believes and says, 'One step enough for me, if Thou, kindly Light, lead on.' The conscious passage from Nature to Nature's God is sacramental in linking the human soul in intimacy and life with the Eternal Maker and Preserver. The greatest and best of our race know and have known by rapturous experience in thought, in vision, in dream, by touch, by hearing, of Heavenly things and of God Most High. For those who have not had this experience to deny it is to assert a fallacy: that the greatest thinkers were fools the greatest; and the most truthful men the worst of liars. The character of Christ is itself enough to brand all gainsayers with infamy.

Advanced science regards the visible glories of Nature as relatives of the invisible powers making them. The temporal present illustration is not the first, nor is it the last: others will follow. The past, in some form, is in the now. The now, in some form, will characterize the future. We cannot think of Almightiness coming to weakness in any of His works; nor of the Eternal dying in any timely arrangements.

The Doctrine of Continuance links all variety to some reality of existence. Eternal significance impresses infinite results as the evergrowing signal of that which seems even the very least in power and meaning. What then can limit the destinies of man, who is so magnificent? His inner unseen majesty is so marvellous that the brain of a few inches in volume pictures, measures, scientifically arranges all worlds. The sacramental grace is Divine.

In many beautiful facts and thoughts, the writer of this book so enforces the truth, that a child may know a Divine achievement is around us; that the differences of form working variety, as they are in relation to and governed by the whole, are under Supreme Rule. All spaces, all times, all phenomena, are for places, durations, structures, further on.

The greatest effort of advanced science is the giving of this greatest proof. God is in all, and will not lose a fraction of that all.

The Great Procession

Is the passage of the powers of the invisible world into manifestation by the visible, and the return, not with loss, but gain. Darkness and Light are both emblems of the greater darkness and the greater light : the invisible is immeasurably greater and more wonderful than the visible. The procession has a benediction progressing to more and more glory. Our fears, our hopes are an admonishment.

That which Christ was, and then became for our sakes, and that which men are, show the tragedy of life as represented in scenes of sin and death. War in Heaven represents an earlier origin as to Sin than the Temptation in Paradise. What we see in the stars warrants the thought that some things in them were out years before our earth was formed. The One who makes the Great Atonement is so Great that He recovers for ever and ever that which was lost, and so puts every part to rights, that the whole is carried on to renewal. Things and men are entablatures with inscriptions of destiny, not as of bondage—and there is the glory—but as of liberty by the Spirit of God.

The trials, the faith, the graces, the gifts, for discipline and adornment of the Pilgrims; their dwellings and laws, their physical and spiritual parts, progress from the Eucharistic character to that bodily union with Christ the Great Restorer, manifest a Supernatural Power, making our manhood and all our affairs a part of that further Divine transcendental coming of our Lord Jesus to accept and welcome the great procession from earth to Heaven, from Time to Eternity, that He may glorify Himself in all things, and that all things may be glorified in Him.

The Great Kingdom.

The inutility of whatever is done apart from God, the Redeemer; the devilish destruction wrought by war for possession of the earth; the painful trials befalling good men, show that the way of the Cross is our Highway, the King's Road to Heaven. Creation all groaning, and men all enduring the Cross, show how strongly the Evil Prince garrisoned his usurpations; but the drugging, the robbing, the murdering of souls, are being put an end to. The dawn-signs of the Kingdom appear. Even those who teach science backward find that Eternal Power, present everywhere, is a Supernatural Presence, filling noble souls, pure hearts, saintly lives, with blissful rest and jubilant expectation.

Nations in their rise and fall, cities in building and in ruins, tell of efforts and failures, of struggles by all for the desired and permanent Kingdom. Meanwhile wheat and tares, good and evil, demons like demagogues, grow and struggle; but, alas! evil ones, their hearts failing through fear, and cursing God, die. The Lord Jesus is yet, so to speak, in humility with us. The great Kingdom is being established in the hearts of those who are content to share His lowliness, and account the shadow of His Cross, and the bearing the lighter part of it, a glory—not shame. They know that the manifestation draweth nigh when they will be priests and princes in the presence of God. Every natural thing is the surface-form of that which is vaster than time. Every token of the Holy Spirit in us is part of a life that death cannot touch. All the willing are being made by faith and prayer, by sanctification, and by use of holy ceremonies to partake sensibly of the Divine Nature. They enter the Kingdom by the Kingdom entering them.

This work in individual hearts, the individuals forming households—the family Church; these meeting in assemblies of the people—the national —the country's Church ; these all of one essential Faith preached unto all nations—the Universal Church, are the Body of Christ in its members, small and great; the particular visible and invisible Church of which He is the Head; of which He is the central Life, nearer to us than our own soul, for He is the Life of that soul; and so wonderfully not only Saviour of the individual body and

Church, but of the great body, the great Church, to be the Shekinah of the Divine glory in the coming kingdom. Meanwhile as angels ministered to Christ they are sent forth as ministering spirits to children of the Kingdom. They bear souls to Paradise. The Book of Revelation tells how these spirits have new names; receive a white stone as an imperishable token of being in covenant, and their songs seem to sound in our ears during those blissful moments in which we realize that already is the kingdom within. Within some little time known to the Lord there will be a wonderful manifestation to the sons of God of the greatness and the everlastingness of His kingdom and theirs.

Pleasant all through is this little book with men beautiful in humility and glorious in exaltation, with God supremely blessed and blessing: the music of the spheres attuned, and everything that hath breath giving praise. May the writer of the book, and every reader of it, take part in all, and dwell with the King of kings and Lord of lords!

CHAPTER I.

THE REALITY OF THE SUPERNATURAL.

WHEN the veil which seems to separate the seen from the unseen is raised by a revelation from God to man, or becomes more transparent by reason of the light shed abroad by the Holy Scriptures, by the discoveries of science, or by a study of man, glorious visions of the world which is invisible to that wonderful instrument the human eye are spread out before us, clear as the sun. Those visions are not, as some profess to believe, like the mirage of the desert; they are realities, more real and enduring than the substantial things of the material world in which we now live.

What is man? Let him stand forth as God made him, with a halo around him of intense white light issuing from the Source of light. We shall see that he is a tripartite being, consisting of body, animal soul, and spirit. The spirit, or spiritual body, is the soul's indissoluble companion, and together they make the 'inner man.' In this lies the man's personality, his individual identity, whether in the natural body or out of it. When death sets free the soul and the spirit from that part of man which is subject to corruption, each man in his distinctive personality, though under altered conditions, goes forth into another stage of existence.

In the mantle of clay that has fallen from him, there is, however, a germ which will at the appointed time burst into life, and unfold into the etherealized resurrection-body; and so in all points the risen man will become like unto his Lord, who returned, after preaching to the spirits in prison, to put on again the body in which He had suffered on the Cross. As that body was changed in its character when raised from the tomb, so will the bodies of those who sleep in Jesus, and the bodies of the saints who are alive on the earth at the second coming of Christ, be changed.

We must go to God's great book of Nature to learn how what seems impossible to man is possible to God; and how, by the working of His unchangeable laws, the millions who have lived and died as the ages have rolled on, and whose mortal bodies have been resolved into their original elements, will nevertheless be, throughout eternity, their own identical selves as truly as those whose bodies will be suddenly changed and caught up to meet the Lord in the air. We drop an acorn into the earth knowing that the life within it will be cherished there, and find expansion in the unfolding of the oak; and so our bodies are committed to the grave in sure and certain hope of a joyful resurrection. It is an old and beautiful belief that each person has his own guardian angel, and as we are told that the angels are ministering spirits sent forth to minister to them who shall be heirs of salvation, it may be that to their care the Great Father has committed the germ of the resurrection-body. Are they not the 'reapers' at the end of the world?

It is often when hope grows dim, when health fails, when a sense of lost opportunities brings a dark shadow over the present, and when, as is sometimes the case, a look back into the past makes the spirit fear to look forward into the future, that the veil is rent by the mercy of God, and we see and feel that our life on earth is but the beginning of our existence, and that all we can learn here below—no matter to what heights we may attain in the search after knowledge—only enables us to see as through a glass darkly, unless light from the Father of Light opens to us what lies beyond the veil. Then it is that things temporal find their true place in the estimation of man, a being who was created for eternity. In this world he is being moulded and trained; in the next he will be what the deeds done in the body have made him, and he will occupy the place for which those deeds have fitted him.

An illustration of the distinction between the higher and lower parts of man's nature, as well as of their close union, may be found in the narrative of the conversion of St. Paul. When the great light from the Sun of Righteousness shone upon him, as he journeyed to Damascus, it blinded him. The veil was then upon his heart, and he was walking in darkness; but the light that blinded him to the things of earth, and closed his mortal eyes to the familiar objects of sight, shone upon the 'inner man,' and showed him that the Flesh pierced by nails and lance on the Cross of Calvary was the tabernacle of Deity—the *veil* which, when torn and lacerated, opened to man 'the new and living way consecrated for us.'

Nearly two thousand years have passed since the veil that rested on the Old Testament Scriptures, which prophesied of the Redeemer of mankind, was raised by their fulfilment in the person of Christ. He came, as the prophets of God said He would, to His people Israel, to 'His own'; but they 'received Him not,' for their materialistic views were as a thick cloud before their eyes, and they could not see their King behind the veil of flesh which He took in order to live among them as a man. They looked for an earthly monarch who should raise them to honour and glory among the nations, and make them rulers in the material universe. They, like the materialists of to-day, cared more for the visible world than for the invisible. They lived for what they saw, and what their hands could handle, and so they could not then, even as men cannot now, see behind the veil.

As time rolls on, man's knowledge seems to make the veil grow thicker as well as broader, and now, at this latter end of the nineteenth century, the world will believe in nothing that is not on this side of the veil, and within reach of man's unaided intellect. Yet it is as true as it ever was, that the 'natural man receiveth not the things of the Spirit of God: for they are foolishness unto him; neither can he know them, because they are spiritually discerned. But he that is spiritual discerneth all things.' Still the natural man walks on, content with the light that his own intellect has kindled. He gazes upon the things which are 'seen and temporal,' until he persuades himself that the things which are 'not seen' and are eternal, are but 'myths' of the 'dark ages.' Unbelief concerning things behind the veil, things 'supernatural,' is oftentimes an outcome of antagonism to religion; but such unbelief is as unnatural as it is unscientific and illogical. It is unnatural because the untaught savage has some sense of spiritual things, however debased it may be; it is unscientific, because almost every new discovery of science proves the existence of unseen power and design; it is illogical, because all that is seen is deducible from, and controlled by, the unseen.

A *savant* of this century has said, 'If men would but give for one century the same amount of effort, time, and labour to the moral sciences and study of the soul, which for the last two centuries they have bestowed upon the physical and natural sciences and mathematics, what marvellous and unforeseen results might be obtained! If men did but perceive ever so faintly, concerning the soul, that which science is beginning to discover as to the astronomical constitution of the universe—viz., that it is a vast, invisible, central world, taking a visible shape in some of its results, which sooner or later will solve many an enigma—and were we less superficial in our meditations, we might obtain some insight as to what is to be found in the depths of the soul, in those vast invisible depths which we too studiously shun, into which we too often refuse even to cast a glance. The farther natural science advances, the more richness, beauty, harmony, the more wondrous results, worthy of God's hand, it discovers in the visible world; and surely there would be a like result in spiritual science. They who seek to explore its depths will assuredly find that those mental regions with which we are familiar are shallow waters as compared therewith.'

When, as is the case in these modern days, men of high culture, who are gifted with unusual intellectual capacities, and who lead irreproachable lives, divorce religion from science, we can but wonder at the power of evil. Those who have eyes to see that there are two worlds which have one supreme Ruler, stand aghast at the theory promulgated in this age of the world's history, that the universe may have sprung into existence without a sentient Maker, and that reasonable beings, evidently made to exercise dominion upon earth, are without a reasonable Ruler. To compare great things with small, we may say that the universe without a God is what man would be without a head. Man, minus a brain, what is he? An idiot asylum gives the answer. Creation robbed of its God is truth eclipsed, a diamond suddenly become dark, space without a pole-star; and man, the crown of creation, a being without anchor, rudder, or compass; a being endowed with free will, dominion and power, yet a mystery to himself in life, and in death a stranded wreck upon the shore of time. That ignorance should lead to unbelief in the existence and creating power of the 'unknown God' should surprise no one. That knowledge, acquired by studying a universe which in every part bears proof of design, and of adaptation to the requirements of organic life, should fail to recognise a Designer, is truly marvellous. In the place of God, some great leaders of modern thought, men of lofty intellect, would put a 'primordial vapour.' They dethrone the Monarch and point to a vacant throne. So men who do not look behind the veil imagine a vacuum; for them there is no supreme good, no fixed standard of right and wrong, no Governor, no infallible Guide; they choose to be a law unto themselves. Hence the anarchy and confusion which are seen everywhere in the world of human thought. As faith dies out, and reason, no longer guided by the light of conscience, is used only to prove that man is an irresponsible being—when, in short, man becomes the slave of his own intellect—he loses the freedom which he might enjoy as a son of God, as made in the image of God. But he does not know this. He sees that his body is fearfully and wonderfully made, noble in design, beautiful in form, and perfectly adapted to all the wants and requirements of his present existence, though it is but a clod of earth when that which he calls '*life*' passes from it. Rather than believe in what he cannot *see*, he is content to let death be, as it were, the coping-stone of the structure which he has raised.

The failure to recognise an intelligent Ruler of reasonable beings is doubtless one cause of the increasing difficulties with which statesmen have to deal, and of the growing evils which perplex the philanthropist. The agnosticism of the present age, in casting the dark shadow of unbelief over the revelation which God has given to man, is sapping the foundation of all social and moral order; and the crude theories of men are set up in the place of eternal truth. In all this is seen the fulfilment of prophecy, which 'sure word' predicts the increase of knowledge 'even to the time of the end.' The New Testament tells of love grown cold, of faith eclipsed in the latter days, and of the second Advent of Christ; just as the Old Testament foretold the falling away of the Jews, their fate among the nations, and the first advent of Christ. The veil that hid the Messiah from the eyes of the Jews, and prevented their seeing in Jesus of Nazareth the fulfilment of prophecy, is the veil that now prevents the great mass of mankind from discerning the 'signs of the times,' and from believing in the reality of the unseen world. It is strange that knowledge which accomplishes such great things, and soars so high, should fail to pierce the veil through which wisdom sees so clearly. Angels might weep when science, which should be the handmaid of religion, severs the bond that unites them; for then the veil becomes so dark that even when the materialistic astronomer rises above the earth, and makes the stars prove the inspiration of the Bible, he fails to realize the significance of his own intellectual achievement, and knows as little of what he has done as did the Jews when they crucified their Messiah.

Alcyone, the supposed centre of gravity of our solar system, and the brightest of the seven bright stars which form the group called by the Greeks 'the Pleiades,' still rolls on, exercising the tremendous force which draws our system around it, at the rate of 422,000 miles a day, in an orbit which it will take thousands of years to complete. This, science may by-and-by proclaim as an ascertained fact, and thus unconsciously teach what is involved in the simple question put by the Creator and Ruler of Alcyone to His servant Job: 'Canst thou bind the sweet influences of Pleiades [Cima]?' That old Chaldean word Cima, meaning a hinge, axle, or pivot, is, like all original words, full of meaning. Suns and worlds revolve around that cluster of stars, whose rising and setting indicated to the sailors of ancient Greece when they might undertake a voyage with safety, and so they called the Cima of the Chaldees the 'Pleiades.' If no other question had been put to Job to impress upon him the difference between the finite understanding of man and the infinite mind of the Creator, the light which science has cast upon the vastness of God's power as declared in this sentence would have been enough to make man feel his own nothingness, and bow down and worship Him whose ways are past finding out.

The wisest and most cultured men of this age, who hold that creation has an intelligent Creator, regard every new discovery of science as a sacred thing—a part of the Temple of Truth. Every new fact that is elicited by patient investigation is received as an important addition to the building, for the simple reason that there is so strong an affinity between science and religion, such an intimate union of the spirit and the body, that sooner or later the material and the immaterial will be recognised as one harmonious whole, at least by those who do not allow their theories to override facts. The value of the bodily senses in investigating truth cannot be over-estimated; and it must always be borne in mind that it is on the evidence of the senses, as well as through revelation, that the belief in the 'supernatural' is maintained. It may be an easy thing for a man to deny the existence of things which he has never seen, but it is not easy to convince a man who has looked through a telescope that there are no stars in space but those which can be seen by his naked eye. How much, it may be asked, would the great mass of mankind know on any subject if they only received what should be demonstrated to each person individually? One who knew nothing of chemistry would deny the presence of any solid substance in two perfectly clear fluids; but a chemist might convince him that solid matter was there by mixing the two fluids, and these, acting upon each other, would cause the solid matter held in solution to be precipitated, and form a dense substance. In that case the evidence of the bodily senses would put an end to incredulity; and why should not the evidence of those senses be received when they testify to supernatural appearances and incidents, which honest and critical observers believe to be as real as any natural object? On other subjects there would be accorded, by those who did not feel able at once to believe, a deferred judgment, an exhaustive inquiry, and at least a provisional verdict; but in the case of the supernatural, evidence that would be deemed conclusive in relation to any other subject is set aside as illusive; there is a contemptuous dismissal of the whole matter, with a condemnation of its advocates. When a clever man of science announces the results of his study to the world, all who are ignorant of the subject, and who have neither the talent nor the opportunity to acquire the necessary knowledge, agree to receive his statements, and they bow down before the might of his intellect. A geologist does not dispute the correctness of the calculations of an astronomer; nor does an astronomer doubt the truth of a geologist's statements. Both know and admit that each must understand the subject which he has made his special study better than one who has been seeking knowledge of another kind, in a different part of the great field of the universe. In days when the increasing light of knowledge should cause prejudice to disappear as stars before the rising sun, those who have made psychology their study ought to be met on the same ground. Ignorance of a subject which gives man higher hopes, clears away some of the mists and vapours that hang about him in this lower stage of existence, and raises the veil that obscures the knowledge of his tripartite nature, is to be deplored, if only because such ignorance must keep men on a low level, from which clearer light and advancing knowledge would raise them.

It would be deeply interesting to know the source of the truths that Homer and Virgil embodied in their verse, and whence they derived their ideas of the spirit world. Later on Dante takes up the theme. Through all the dreams of the writers of the classic epics there is to be traced the one key-note. The foundation-stone of the elaborate column which each great poet has raised is the same, and it is the same as that found in the sacred poetry of the Jews. It is more clearly developed in the words and acts of Him who was crucified on Calvary, and still further elaborated in the Pauline Epistles. Around the one mysterious truth which enters into all mental superstructures there have clustered an ever-increasing number of related truths. They come from the unseen world—they testify to the reality of that world. Thus has faith been kept alive and strengthened; and thus, from time to time, have the minds of men been led towards the borders of the spirit-land, where, resting for awhile, they have learned much that, in the rush and hurry of the world, they could not have otherwise learned.

It is a great mistake to think, as so many appear to do, that but little is revealed to us in the Holy Scriptures of the invisible world and its inhabitants. All that anyone, who regards man's short life on earth as a preparation for a higher state of existence, can want to know is plainly stated. He is told that the invisible part of his nature is immortal, clothed for a time with a mortal body, which he is to care for and keep undefiled until the moment arrives when he must leave it, and go to the place for which the deeds done in the body have fitted him. He is told that good and evil are in the world, and that, having been made in the image of God, he is capable of knowing what is right and what is wrong, and that he is free to choose the good and to refuse the evil. He is told that there are evil spirits under the dominion of a great fallen archangel, and that these tempt men to sin. Also that there are good angels ever ministering to him, influencing his thoughts, protecting him in the midst of unseen dangers, and warding off evil. Incidents illustrating these truths are to be found in all parts of the inspired writings, and anyone who will open his Bible, and, with the help of a concordance, carefully read, cannot fail to apprehend something of that invisible world in which man is a great central figure. He belongs to two worlds—two, yet one—the visible and the invisible, the material and the spiritual. Such an earnest and sincere reader will find himself in the position of a mountaineer who, after toiling up a steep ascent from some low land, reaches a plateau on which he can rest awhile, and study the wonders and glories of the hitherto unknown region that is spread out before him. There he may learn that the inhabitants of the 'unseen world' have organisms like his own. The nature, the office, the duties, and the characteristics of the holy angels are minutely described by an unerring guide, who shows him how, when the first Adam fell, angels barred the way back to Eden with their flaming swords; how they sang when the Second Adam took our flesh and dwelt among us; how they ministered to Him in the wilderness and in the Garden of Gethsemane; and how they rolled away the stone from the mouth of the sepulchre when He rose victor over death and the grave. Angels were entertained by Abraham, took Lot out of Sodom, and carried the poor man who lay at the gate of Dives to rest in the bosom of Abraham. At the last great day angels are to go forth, as reapers, to separate the tares from the wheat, and they are to accompany the Son of Man when He comes to sit upon the throne of His glory.

Of the angels that sinned it is written, that they were cast down to hell, and delivered into chains of darkness, to be reserved unto judgment; and of those evil spirits that possessed man in the olden time the student learns enough to know that their subtle organisms enable them to enter into man and dwell in him, tempting him to evil, torturing him to madness, and afflicting him with bodily disease.

The starting-point for each individual is his natural birth. Before him are two roads. Evil cannot harm him, or soil his garments, unless he stretches forth his hand and takes it to his bosom, and makes it his own; neither is good forced upon him against his will. He is free, and by his own act stands or falls. Heaven and hell are set before man as the termini of the journey he has to take.

'Once to every man and nation comes the moment to decide
In the strife of Truth with Falsehood for the good or evil side,

Some great cause, God's new Messiah, offering each the
  bloom or blight,
Puts the goats upon the left hand, and the sheep upon the
  right,
And the choice goes by for ever 'twixt that darkness and
  that light.'

But, besides heaven and hell, there is an intermediate state, called Hades, into which man enters when death sets him free from the body. Thither the Lord Jesus went after His decease; and in that part of Hades which is known as Paradise the penitent thief met his Redeemer. It is the place where Abraham, Isaac, and Jacob were located, for of them Jesus said: 'God is not the God of the dead, but of the living.' It is the place where the spirits of just men made perfect rest from their labours; and where the souls of the martyrs, robed in white, wait until the number of the elect is made up. It is the place to which the daughter of Jairus went when death touched her, and whence her spirit came again when He who conquered death called her back to earth. It is the place where the spirits of Lazarus, and of the widow's son, dwelt for a time until the commands 'Arise!' 'Come forth!' were given by Him who holds the keys of Hades. It is the place where the beggar Lazarus was when the rich man, from his place of torment, prayed for a drop of water to cool his tongue. During his trial time on earth Dives had not given, out of the abundance of his wealth, even the crumbs which fell from his table to feed the hungry. He was clothed in purple and fine linen, but he did not clothe the naked; he lived for this world only, and when he had to leave it he found himself far away from the rest and the peace of those who are pronounced 'blessed.' The parable of Dives and Lazarus teaches much more than superficial readers imagine, and it furnishes a most important link in the chain that stretches from the throne of God to His footstool. There is a very general belief—idea would, perhaps, be the better word to use—that there is a sudden change in man at the moment of death. No greater sophism was ever propounded, for, as Bishop Butler says, 'Our organized bodies are no more ourselves or part of ourselves than any other matter around us.' The material body drops off; the dress in which man fights the battle of life wears out and falls to pieces, but the man himself goes forth, in full consciousness and activity, his identity preserved in the spirit frame that environs his soul, with all his senses expanded, and retaining all his old memories. The parable, or, as is very commonly believed, the narrative of two actual lives thus given by Christ, indisputably teaches all this. St. Paul was caught up to the third heaven while his natural body was on earth. On the Mount of Transfiguration Moses and Elias were seen talking to Jesus of His death, which was shortly to be accomplished; and to the dying martyr, St. Stephen, extended power of sight was granted, so that he was enabled to see Jesus 'standing at the right hand of God.'

This is but a small part of what may be gathered from the pages of Revelation on a subject which is of vast importance and supreme interest, but it is more than enough to prove to all who believe that the Bible contains a revelation from God to man, that man's career is a progressive one from the beginning; that he is not left in ignorance of his future condition after his so-called death; that he is, when absent from the body, a conscious, active being, with the same organisms as when in the body, but those organisms so spiritualized that he is not subject to the laws of matter (according to our present knowledge of those laws), and therefore can traverse space, and become visible to mortal vision, and even speak so as to be heard by mortal ear, whenever the Lord wills or permits. Whoever receives the testimony of the Scriptures must admit that what *has been* in one age, *may be* in another, and that all the supernatural events recorded in later times have their prototypes in Scripture narratives.

The elevating effect of a belief in the reality of the supernatural can only be understood by those who have gone to the Fountain of Truth, or have looked beyond the veil; but let any intelligent thinker ask himself, What is left to us when the supernatural element is eliminated? There would then be the material universe, without any great sovereign mind to set each star in its orbit, and to order its course. There would be our planet Earth in motion without any sentient controlling power; and its myriads of human beings coming into existence, to suffer, to sin and to die—to drop into the grave, and in a little while crumble into dust. Many only live to endure toil, poverty and disease; and if there is no ground for the belief in something better and nobler and more enduring than the present life and its surroundings, by what principle of supposed right and wrong can any man be blamed for saying that he has as much right to the good things of this life as his neighbour has?

It may be broadly stated that even the vague, shadowy belief held by the masses, that there are such things as 'ghosts,' 'haunted houses' and 'warnings,' and that when they die they will become angels, and go to some place where cold and hunger will not be felt, where they will be able to rest, is an incalculable good. All this hazy faith, varying in degree according to the weaker or firmer grasp which each individual mind has of the fundamental truth—that there is one great, loving Father of all, who will make the crooked ways smooth, and put all straight some day—maintains things as they are. Eliminate all that the Bible and the

THE REALITY OF THE SUPERNATURAL

Church have taught; all that theologians have believed, and those who have lived holy and useful lives, who have done most good for the poor and for their country, whether as priests, as statesmen, or as soldiers; blot out all superstition, and with it the deep truths which underlie it; and in place of all this give to mankind the creed that some men hold, and a state of chaos would be the result, of which it makes the brain reel to think. The men who believe in nothing but what they see and understand, or think they understand, and whose idea of immortality is that their own knowledge will live on in the minds of those who shall come after them, are comparatively few in number. Their ideas of morality, justice and truth (whence are they derived?), their intellectual pursuits and their cultured tastes, may keep *them* on a high level : but without their knowledge, and also without the faith and hope of the Christian, what must the condition of the masses be? The only logical sequence of unbelief in the supernatural is anarchy and rebellion, each man for himself, the strongest to the fore, the weak to the wall; in a word, the fate which befell old Rome when her citizens lost their faith both in man and in the gods.

It has been the fashion of the nineteenth century to speak of mediæval times as the 'dark ages,' but as a belief in the supernatural lies at the root of all belief in the Christian faith, and as to undermine the one is to destroy the other, future generations will perhaps find, when weighing cause and effect, that the age in which belief in the supernatural degenerated into superstition, formed a brighter epoch in the history of man than the age of reason, which, with all its knowledge and opportunities of finding *Truth* in the light that knowledge kindles, grew morally dark as Faith became eclipsed. As soon as man closes his eyes to all save material things, he is as a caged bird, and the loftiest intellect will not enable him to soar beyond the material network by which he has surrounded himself. Thus he becomes, unconsciously, a living illustration of what Bacon calls 'the apotheosis of error.'

It is admitted by all that a good solid foundation is essential to every building. If the shaft and capital of a column are to stand, the plinth must be immovable. This is a law which admits of no variation in the material world, and it will be found to hold also in the spiritual world. The man who attempts to build up any hypothesis upon other foundation than unalloyed Truth, will sooner or later discover that he has been building upon sand. The superstructure may be beautiful to the eye, and look well in the spring-time of life; it may last while summer lasts, and the slanting rays of the autumnal sun may gild its stones, and cause them to seem what the builder thought they were when he fixed each in its place; but when the winds of winter blow and beat upon it, and rain descends from above, and the floods come, the building falls. A tree is known by its fruit, and it would seem that many who have, during past years, been sowing the seeds of knowledge have not sown in the right soil, for in the rank luxuriance of leaves and blossoms there is an almost universal indication that the fruit will not prove to be good. The seed sown may have been good of its kind, but, lacking the support it needed for its perfect development, its end is withered leaves and cankered blossoms. To drop metaphor, just as man must have a standard by which to measure distances, and to weigh quantities, and as without such a standard there would be no possibility of defining the true and the false, so in morals there must be a fixed standard of right and wrong. That standard can only be fixed by one who is omniscient. Those who know that they are liable to err, even when striving to do what is right, know also that no standard of right and wrong which *they* could set up would stand the test of being examined and dissected by other men; for however exalted the standard might be in the eyes of him who originated it, of others like-minded, or of those on a lower moral and intellectual level, it would fall far short of perfection when the rays of light from a clearer conscience, and a loftier intellect crowned with humility, fell upon it. No man can set up an infallible standard for his fellow-man which all must acknowledge to be the true one, and by which all must be judged; this the God-man alone can do.

All Christians would, of course, receive this proposition without hesitation; but if those who are not Christians would, for the sake of argument, receive it hypothetically, and then work out the problem honestly, Faith and Reason would be found by many of them to be twin stars, each reflecting the light derived from the Source of light. Assuming, then, that there is an unassailable standard of right and wrong, where is it to be found? The answer is, 'In the life of Jesus of Nazareth.' As the accusers of the adulteress disappeared when the words were spoken, 'Let him that is without sin among you first cast a stone at her,' leaving, as St. Augustine says, 'two things alone together, misery and mercy,' so, one by one, each noble soul, no matter what creed is held, must bow down and confess that there is, and must be, something far higher, and purer, and nobler than himself or things around him; something or someone which all that is good and great in his own nature is yearning after. In the history of a world ruined by sin, only one perfect Man has appeared. Pure and undefiled He stands forth, perfect in holiness. While gentle and obedient to man's law, He yet appears on the Mount of Beatitudes as the unerring Lawgiver. From the sepulchre He comes forth as the Victor of Death; and from the heaven to which He has ascended He calls upon his brothers and sisters to follow Him. He is the standard for man, and men will look in vain for another.

When the outlook over the whole civilized world is gloomy, and the dawn of a revolutionary epoch is discernible everywhere; when inch by inch the standard of morality is lowering to suit the tastes and habits of the two extremes of the social scale; when what is expedient in legislation is substituted for what is right; when knowledge that will enable a child to 'get on' in the world is compulsory, and the teaching is withheld which would enable the young and plastic mind to realize that truth is better than falsehood, and honest labour is more honourable than what is designated 'sharp practice,' the primary cause of retrogression is not far to seek. It is found in the fact that man has substituted a lower standard, the outcome of his own knowledge, for the higher standard fashioned by the wisdom of God. The lowering of this standard is but the natural consequence of the non-recognition of the supernatural; for, as has been well said, 'In some sense of the supernatural, in some faith in the unseen, in some feeling that man is not of this world, in some grasp on the Eternal

God, and on an eternal supernatural and supersensuous life, lies the basis of all pity and mercy, all help, and comfort, and patience, and sympathy among men. Set these aside, commit us only to the natural, to what our eyes see and our hands handle, and, while we may organize society scientifically, and live according to "the laws of nature," and be very philosophical and very liberal, we are standing on the ground on which every savage tribe stands, or indeed on which every pack of wolves gallops.'

No one who thinks seriously on this momentous subject can fail to see, that the ultimate issue of the conflict between Christianity and unbelief must turn on the admission or denial of the supernatural, and that such a denial is also a denial of God. But the prayer, 'Father, forgive them, for they know not what they do,' has never ceased, and never will cease, until the last man who is to be saved *is* saved; for the *purpose* of God is unchangeable, and is unaffected by the ebb and flow of man's belief. That purpose is that 'all men shall be saved, and come to the knowledge of the Truth,' as it is in Christ Jesus our Lord. Those who believe in Him who said, 'All shall know Me, from the least even unto the greatest,' look with confidence and joy beyond the present evil days of ignorance and unbelief: they look on to the time of the restitution of all things, knowing that

THE REALITY OF THE SUPERNATURAL

> 'Life is real ! Life is earnest !
> And the grave is not its goal;
> Dust thou art, to dust returnest,
> Was not spoken of the soul.'

They know that although they 'see but dimly through the mists and vapours, amid these earthly damps,' that life beyond the grave is a great reality, and that for man, made in the image of God,

> 'There is no death, what seems so is transition;
> This life of mortal breath
> Is but a suburb of the life elysian,
> Whose portal we call death.'

They know that the time will come when God shall wipe away all tears; and there shall be 'no more death, neither sorrow, nor crying, neither shall there be any more pain.' They look for the new heaven and the new earth; and for the holy city that will have no need of the sun, neither of the moon, to shine in it, for the glory of God will lighten it, and the Lamb will be the light thereof. And so, even while walking through the 'Vale of Tears,' they can lift up their heads and cry: 'O Death, where is thy sting ? O Grave, where is thy victory ?'

The man who realizes that he is an immortal being, immortal because he is the son of Him who is without beginning or end; and that this immortal Father has willed that man shall work with Him in carrying on His great designs in His universe, and has environed him with a body fitted for the work appointed for him to do in this material world, *that* man knows what he is; he grasps his position, and feels its responsibilities; he recognises the self-evident fact that, just as every child should be trained for the position in life on earth which he or she has to occupy—and this life is the school-life, during which the training for higher work takes place—so upon the right use of his own free will, and the cultivation of the talents bestowed upon him, must depend a man's fitness for a more exalted or a lower position in the next stage of his existence. He who aims high, and who allows humility to safeguard his aspirations, brings his body into subjection, fights against sin, wills that the higher part of his nature shall rule the lower, and in so doing brings himself into conformity to the perfect will of God and conquers; yet not in his own strength alone, for the will to work, to obey, and, if need be, to suffer, being also the will of God, is the power of God in man: so that all good is of God.

By making use of 'every good and perfect gift that comes down from the Father of Lights, with whom is no variableness, neither shadow of turning,' man conquers and is crowned; by the disuse or misuse of those gifts and of the opportunities vouchsafed for their employment, he loses his crown; if not entirely and for ever, still there must be loss, because the jewels which can be found and polished only on earth in the strait path of duty will not be set in it. The wisest and best of God's children love to think that the school-life does not end when the worn-out instrument which fitted them for learning and working in a material world is laid aside, and the spirit is set free; for man does but leave the lower form for a higher one, if in this natural life he has been a diligent student. But what will happen if the lessons on the lower form have not been learned? Can they ever be learned? It is a solemn thought. Elementary truths are not taught in the higher school, and so it seems that there must be loss. A lost moment is lost for ever; a lost opportunity can never be won back; the past cannot be recalled. The margin of the great river of Death is reached at last, and whatever the spirit of man has failed to gather up, and place in safe-keeping, will be lacking on the other side of the river. Where there is no sickness and sorrow, no cold and hunger, no nakedness and want, there can be no opportunity for learning many of the lessons taught by the life of Christ on earth. We cannot tell, we do not know, how the neglect of learning lessons here below will tell upon the future. Christ endured the ills and sorrows of life on earth that He might be like us, and teach us how we may be like Him.

Poor, and despised, and rejected, He went about doing good; and if men do not follow in His footprints, they cannot be like their Lord in that respect. Dives did not learn that lesson in this world; and the veil which by infinite wisdom is cast over one part of creation is raised by the God-man, to show men of future generations the result in the next stage of man's existence of not obeying the commands of the great Teacher, and not learning the lessons which the Holy Spirit has always been ready to teach man.

Study of the visible universe, and of the mysteries of the kingdom of Nature, even apart from what is revealed to us of the unseen world, leads the mind almost irresistibly to the conclusion that there must be an Author and Maker of all, from whom all is derived, and in whom is infinite wisdom and power to create, and also to govern and frame laws for the universe. Those laws being the evolution and expression of infinite knowledge, and designed to work in unbroken continuity, must be in perfect harmony, not only with the will of the Lawgiver, but with each other. They must be uniform in their working as applied to both spirit and matter. In man we see the blending together of the material and the immaterial; the body and the spirit that animates, directs, and controls the body. We can clearly discern how any principle which did not work harmoniously with both, would create confusion and disruption. This the sin of man has done. God made man upright; an enemy has caused him to fall from his uprightness. But God's law remains unchanged and unchangeable; and as surely as 'in Adam all die, so in Christ shall all be made alive,' and restored, in God's own time, according to His eternal purpose in Christ Jesus, and by the working of His unchanging law, to the image of God in which man was originally made. The time when the prophecy, 'All shall know Me, from the least unto the greatest,' shall be fulfilled, seems to be very far away, yet it may be nearer than we imagine. We live at a period of the world's history when the spread of knowledge, and with it the estimate of the vastness and power of man's intellectual possibilities, apparently induce men to overlook the fact, that as they never reach a point beyond which there is not a higher, there must be a 'starting point' quite beyond their present grasp; there must be the Origin and Moving Power of all, the Author and Enlightener of intellect; 'the Great First Cause, least understood.' One leader of modern thought has said that 'religion is evolved by a process of naturalistic development, the first term of which was a primitive man's shadow, and the last, God, the Maker of heaven and earth, and Judge of all mankind.' This, however, is unsatisfactory, even from the writer's own point of view; for there is the *fact of sin*, and the phenomena of *conscience;* and, face to face with these, the theory of the evolution of religion by a process of naturalistic development breaks down, for it has no base, no starting-point. The 'inner man' has at once to confront two facts which cannot be accounted for, save by the acknowledgment of a revelation from some higher power. That power has always been felt by man. God has never left man without a witness, though He only revealed Himself fully in the person of Jesus Christ. Pilate asked the question, 'What is Truth?' The answer he received was not in words, but in the silent, majestic presence of 'The Truth' in its fulness. But truth is a many-sided thing, and man, who sees only in part, grasps one phase or another, and then, giving the reins to his imagination, fashions a religion of his own; in this way it comes about that there are many 'faiths' in the world. Or a man closes his eyes to all but the creations of his own brain, and puts altogether away from him the revealed Truth. For these persons the Christian can only feel infinite pity, which—when combined with admiration for the splendid talents that so often accompany scepticism and infidelity, and for the unfailing perseverance with which these students of nature pursue the course on which they have entered—deepens as the thought comes home to the believer that 'the things which are seen are temporal; but

THE REALITY OF THE SUPERNATURAL

the things which are not seen are eternal'; for he knows that when the Angel of Death sets him free from his earthly tabernacle, the light of an unsetting sun will shine upon him, and he will 'know even as he is known'; whereas the unbeliever in God and immortality leaves doubt, and the shadows of time, for the deeper shadows of Hades, where the knowledge will come to him, as it came to Dives, that he had missed the mark of his high calling, and must pay the penalty for despising his birthright, and making no use of opportunities which, once lost, are lost for ever.

The more deeply we meditate upon the effect which loss of faith in the reality of the unseen world has upon the character of man, the more important it appears to be to use every effort to bring back into the world the clear, firm faith of an earlier age, and to show to all who are seeking truth that visions of the unseen, and so-called immaterial, world are not myths and delusions, but realities, more lasting than the things we see around us, for *they* perish in the using: matter is resolved into its primary elements; spirit is not subject, so far as man knows, to laws which govern the material world. Hence it is that the witness of God's truth on earth—the Catholic and Apostolic Church—lives, and lives to render its witness. The Church lives, because the Spirit that giveth life dwells in it, and abides with it for ever. Man may mar the outward and visible form, but he cannot rob the Church of that inward and spiritual grace which is its own, by reason of union with the Head, and which gives and sustains that inherent power which renders it invulnerable. Man may seem to wound and crush it, but he cannot destroy its vitality. With the world against it, and the powers of darkness leagued together to destroy the Church, it is safe, and stands secure amid the storms of time, a monument of its founder's power. It may appear to be rent asunder by the heresies and sins of men, but being one with the Lord, and one in 'the faith once for all delivered,' which is summed up in the Creed of the Universal Church, and sealed by the last Œcumenical Council, it is, as it has been, and as it ever will be, one and indivisible; its members sons and daughters of the great universal Father, brothers and sisters of the 'Word that was made flesh, and dwelt among us.'

When Christ took our nature upon Him, He united the material and the immaterial, the natural and the spiritual, even as God in the beginning united them, when He made man. It is difficult to understand how those who believe Christ to be God Incarnate can regard the Church as merely a human institution. If Christ be God as well as man, the Divine and the human in one Person, His Church must also be divine and human, not only as being one corporate body, but divine and human in each individual member of that body. When man fails to realize this fact, he cannot see the Holy Spirit sanctifying the waters of baptism, or the hidden God of the Eucharist on the altars of His Church, because these things are spiritually discerned by that higher part of his being which, to all who do not intelligently believe in the reality of the Unseen, is simply *something* that they cannot understand. They see a brother die. They know that the body lying cold and stiff and motionless will soon crumble to dust; but what has become of all that made the man? Gone *somewhere*. What was the *something* that animated the clay image, soon to be laid in the grave? Alas! all behind the veil is shadowy and unreal to him who has not an intelligent grasp of the duality of his own nature. One who has that grasp, when he sees the head bowed or the knee bent at the name of Jesus, sees only an evidence of spirit moving matter—the unseen controlling the seen. When he sees the sign of the Cross made, he regards it as an outward sign of the willingness of the 'inner man' to be as his Master, and to take up his cross and follow that Master. When he sees a brother or sister kneel before the Blessed Sacrament, he knows that in body and in spirit worship is offered to the Creator and Saviour of both. With the heart man believeth; with the mouth he confesses his belief. When the heart is merry, a smile plays about the lips and gladness is heard in the voice; when it is sad, tears glisten in the eye and a sigh or a moan is breathed forth. One man who has much knowledge of the material universe deems it wisdom to ignore one part of his being; another, who knows himself, knows also that what is behind the material veil is of more value than the mortal environment, which does but enable him to work here on earth, and falls from him when the earth-work is done.

The hazy faith, if faith it may be called, which prevents so many professing Christians from seeing anything clearly that is beyond human sight, causes them to regard themselves as mere denizens of earth, and the Church as a valuable teacher of ethics. She is to them a good and useful institution, and she is nothing more. They see that part of her which is on this side of the veil, and dream not of what lies on the other side. They see the base of the 'pillar and ground of the truth,' and a certain portion of her shaft, but her capital is beyond their ken. The dense atmosphere of this world hides the light and life of the Church from all who only regard the surface of things, but those who look below the surface see the Church on earth battling with the powers of evil—sorrowful, yet always rejoicing; persecuted, afflicted, tormented, yet overcoming evil with good; returning blessing for cursing; beaten back from point to point, but never yielding; her flagstaff sometimes broken, but her colours never taken. Her members fight against the god of this world and his hosts, and the world deems them powerless, because it does not see the One, far above all rule, and authority, and power, and dominion, who is their strength and their leader, to whom they are indissolubly united. The world thinks that the Catholic and Apostolic Church, in her divine aspect, is a myth, and that the faith of the Church is a delusion; but her members know that their hopes are fixed upon a building not made with hands, eternal in the heavens, and based upon the 'Rock of Ages.' They know that the centre of their faith is the Alpha and Omega of the Church—the, at present, invisible Head of the mystical body, which He has purchased for Himself, and which He and His co-workers are directing and controlling, just as the spirit of man directs and controls his body. This fact, taught by revelation, received by faith, and confirmed by reason, is enough for those who can distinguish 'truth and error.' If, in a general sense, Pilate's question, 'What is truth?' is asked, the answer is plain. It is what science is, accurate knowledge, the opposite of falsehood, which is the denial of truth. It follows, therefore, that there can be no falsehood where there is no truth—there can be no denial of what *is not*.

It would not be easy for an unbeliever in the unseen world, and its spiritual inhabitants, to give a satisfactory reason for all the rhetoric that in these days is employed to stamp out belief in the supernatural, or to explain why men spend time and employ their talents to destroy a nonentity. They must admit the universality of the belief in supernatural power and manifestations, for it has always existed, in every age and in every clime, as it exists to-day among all nations, and it is as much a part of the creed of learned men of the nineteenth century as it was of men who saw the dead raised by Him who 'brought life and immortality to light,' and who told them of their home above, and the many mansions in His Father's house. The thought of immortality elevates the mind, and he who meditates on the meaning of the word 'eternity,' is not likely to confine all his aspirations to time, or concentrate his thoughts upon earth. He who is content to be 'a giant' on earth must be also content to see nothing but the sphere around him. He cannot, from his own point of view, raise himself or others ; and we cannot but believe that there are moments when our greatest materialistic teachers would give all their boasted knowledge for an unwavering faith in immortality, when in their inmost being they feel what the late Poet Laureate has embodied in the pathetic words,

> 'Oh for the touch of a vanished hand,
> The sound of a voice that is still !'

THE REALITY OF THE SUPERNATURAL

They would welcome the faintest gleam of light from the world they ignore, if it showed them that the loved and lost to mortal sight were only behind a veil, safe for ever in the hand of a God of love.

The position taken by men who reject Revelation, and with it dogmatic theology, appears to the ordinary mind as untenable as it is illogical; for while treating any allusion to the supernatural with supercilious contempt, they have themselves gathered from the region of metaphysics all the power that enables them to unlock the mysteries of the kingdom of Nature, to understand the working of the laws which govern it, and to adapt its treasures to the use of man. There is also a very important, because practical, bearing which the non-recognition of the supernatural has upon the lives of men. It is impossible for any deep thinker, who is an observer of the present conditions of social and political life in these closing years of the nineteenth century, not to feel that a crisis in the history of the world is approaching—a crisis evolved out of the actions of men, those actions being but the embodiment of all the brain-power which is exercised so freely for good or evil in this age of reason. It is also impossible to avoid coming to the conclusion that the ground on which previous generations have stood, or thought they stood, secure, is crumbling away beneath their feet, and that they must slide down the steep grade with the multitude, or they must climb to higher ground, and find some rock on which they can feel safe, and live for nobler ends than the great majority dream of.

There is a general longing for a better and higher life than has been realized by man on earth since the fall, and this is evidenced by the work of those whose lives prove that they deem no sacrifice too great, if, by immolating self, they can raise their fellow-men from the depths of sin and suffering into which they have fallen. But the lost sheep are many and the shepherds are few—so few that if we had not the great historical drama of Christianity shining out of the darkness, and the Author and Chief Actor in the drama standing alone in a world arrayed against Him, we should marvel at the work which they accomplish. The secret of their success is to be found in the fact that, having followed in the steps of the ideal man, Christ Jesus, of Him in whom His bitterest enemies could 'find no fault,' their work is based upon a sure foundation, that foundation being absolute truth. This unquestionable fact accounts for the triumphant march of Christianity. Its Founder died the death of a malefactor. He was rejected, reviled, crucified, and yet came off more than conqueror. So it is with His servants, and the adversary has no more power to overthrow them and their work than he had when he tempted

Christ, and was foiled by Him. If we take a practical view of the principles upon which the social and political life of nations and individuals rests, it will be seen that the foundation which supports Christianity is not the base on which the world's principles are built. Therefore the actions in which the world's principles are embodied are always shifting, and the history of the world, as illustrated by the rise and fall of nations, is not a record of steady growth, but of alternating progression and retrogression. Everywhere men are clamouring for change. There is no fixity of purpose, no cohesion of the conflicting elements which every year increase the gigantic warlike armaments that are necessary, it is said, to preserve peace among nations. That statement is in itself a proof that 'there is something rotten in the state of Denmark.' Truth has a coherent power in itself; it is steadfast and immovable, and all that is based upon it makes for peace and not for war. It creates order, not confusion, and the light that radiates from it dispels the mists and vapours which in every age have gathered round the false.

If proof were needed of the imminent danger of elevating a false standard, we have but to glance at the history of democracy on the one hand, and of autocracy on the other; for both are subversive of the golden rule, 'Do unto others as you would have others do unto you.' The two extremes meet, and the autocrat and the democrat are scarcely divided in principle by a hair's breadth. The social democrat would lower everything to his own level, and the autocrat would do the same. Each would be guided by the same principle—that of subjugating all to his own will. The problem to be solved is not an easy one, unless in answering the question, 'What *is* to be done when all men are agitating for change'? we go back to first principles, and start afresh on the basis of truth. In order to make this possible man must be taught to know himself, and to realize that he *is* something more than that which he *seems to be;* and that there is a purpose for his being, and a work for him to do, for which this life is preparing him. The moment a human being faces the questions, 'Whence came I?' 'What am I?' 'Where do I go?' he is compelled against his will to admit that, apart from Revelation, his only answer to the first and last questions must be, 'I do not know.' To the middle question the only answer he could give would be, 'I am a man.' Then arises the question, 'What is man?' The Holy Scriptures, which agnostics regard as fables, tell us what man is, whence he came, why he is placed in this great earthly school, and whither he will go when his lessons are learned. Again, if the question, 'What is man?' is asked of history, the answer is given by pointing to Christ; to His words, His works, His life from the cradle to the cross. He is the perfect Man, the express image of the Father, and because He is Man, He claims us for His own, and, fallen as we are, He calls us His 'brother,' and 'sister,' and 'mother.' Nay, more, his 'bride,' for whom He laid down His life. Ask of one who never heard of Christ, or who, having heard, has rejected Him, 'What is man?' and he can but point to himself, to his wonderfully-made body, which is soon to be resolved into the elements out of which it was framed. There is no past, no future. He is what he is for a moment of time. He may be a giant in intellect, a model of morality, a lover of all that is great and good; he may be a favourite of fortune, a king among men, or he may be the opposite of all this, born into the world only to suffer. What in either case does it matter when the decree goes forth, 'Ashes to ashes, dust to dust'? If no part of man is immortal, it is better for him never to have been.

If man would learn to know himself first, and that part of the universe which is within reach of his limited faculties next, there would be less agnosticism and more wisdom, less pride and more humility; for knowledge of self, while showing man his transcendent greatness and his limitless capabilities, as made in the image of God, also teaches him his infinite littleness in his fallen state, and shows him what the higher part of his nature, the 'inner man,' has to do during the school life of earth, before he can recover all that for him Adam lost. To do this he must keep up a continual warfare against sin, for though Christ, by the sacrifice of Himself as man, has redeemed man, and opened for him a new and living way to heaven, man has now, as in old time, to choose the good and refuse the evil; in short, he must work out his own salvation in God's appointed way. It is man's high privilege to be a worker *with* God, not a machine worked *by* God; otherwise man would be little more than a pen in the hand of the writer, or the clod beneath his feet. The great need of the present day is a realization of the fact, that what is called 'the supernatural' is as real as the natural, and that the visible universe is but the embodiment of God's mind, just as music and painting are the embodiments of man's thoughts. Words are, after all, but clumsy things, but we have to use them. They serve our purpose well as long as they treat of the visible and material world, but the moment we touch the great unseen world, words fail us. We only know what electricity is by its effects; we make use of what we cannot see, we grasp what we cannot feel. We live and move and have our being by a power of which we know nothing—a power or principle which we can control and subjugate to our will, and so far it is our own. We know that it *is*; but the *cause* is known to God only. It is an extension of His own life-giving and creative power, and the fact that it is of Him, and from Him, making us one with Him, constitutes our greatness. The knowledge of this fact must tend to make man feel that he is a responsible being, created not for time only but also for eternity, and until men and women are taught to know themselves, and to realize their position in creation, individuals and nations will live and act for this world only. The ruler of the powers of darkness knows well that he can best succeed in deceiving man by leading him to ignore and to deny the unseen, and to believe only in what he can see and understand; thus losing sight of who and what he really is. As sons of God men belong to two worlds, the material and the so-called, by way of distinction, immaterial. While incarnate they have to do with the material world in which for a few years they live and work; and if they realized, as God would have them do, that the 'inner man' controls and regulates the outer man, and lives on when the other dies, they would soon cease to scoff at the supernatural as but a phantasy of the diseased brain, and at the belief in it as only a deteriorating superstition.

CHAPTER II.

THE GREAT SACRAMENT—GOD IN NATURE.

A GREAT sacrament is a great mystery. When God willed the union of spirit and matter, He embodied His creative power in countless organisms during the successive ages which are referred to in the first book of Holy Scripture. Through those ages each chapter of the Book of Nature was developed from the minutest particle of which matter is composed until the work of creation was finished, and was declared by the Creator to be 'very good.' Order had taken the place of chaos. Earth, and sea, and sky were fashioned after the mind of the great Artificer. Suns and stars were set in the firmament. The fowls of the air, the fishes of the sea, and the beasts of the earth were made; and then the Council of the Trinity decreed that man should be created in the image of God, and that he should be lord of creation, and have dominion over all the earth. When the heavens and the earth were finished, and all the host of them, and God saw that all was good, and that His work of creation was ended, He rested from all His work which He had made. It was all perfect then, and all His work is perfect now ; for God is as unchangeable in His works and purpose as He is unchangeable in Himself. Every page of the Book of Nature tells only of perfection—perfection in the smallest as in the greatest things. Man speaks of things as being 'great' and 'small,' but when he finds in the minutest atom which the most powerful microscope can show him a perfect adaptation to place and use, and sees in the smallest organism as much design as in what man calls the 'noblest works in creation,' he can but feel that there is nothing really great or small in God's sight. God made and sustains everything. The smallest crystal in the granite rock, the mote seen in the sunbeam, are as truly maintained in their position by Almighty Power as are the stars in their orbits ; and man is taught that, as concerning his body, the hairs of his head are numbered, and as concerning the divine part of his nature, that he can be enlightened and guided by the Holy Spirit. 'Oh, the depth of the riches both of the wisdom and knowledge of God! How unsearchable are His judgments, and His ways past finding out.' ' Lord, what is man that Thou art mindful of him, and the son of man that Thou visitest him ? For

Thou hast made him a little lower than the angels, and hast crowned him with glory and honour. Thou madest him to have dominion over the works of Thy hands; Thou hast put all things under his feet.'

God had sown good seed in the field of the universe, but an enemy sowed tares among the wheat. Evil entered the garden, and the trail of the serpent blighted the fairest flowers. From the moment that God breathed life into the human frame which He had made, man became a living soul; and then evil, the opposite of good, strove, and has striven through the ages, to prevent the union of spirit and matter, and to break off the relations between man and his Maker. Evil has so far succeeded as to make the history of man on earth appear to be a series of damaged links, though the golden chain of Divine love still binds the creature to his Creator.

When contemplating the material universe as the outward and visible sign of the Creator, man begins to know himself. He may learn, in the presence of the 'Great Sacrament,' what he is, as the crown of creation and the son of God. His mortal body is a temple in which the Holy Ghost may dwell. It is the Spirit of God which enables man to rejoice in the glories around him in nature, and causes a thrill of pleasure to pass through his being when some harmonious chord is heard.

Man may realize that though disease and death destroy the material part of his nature, they cannot touch the divine part. Nevertheless the spirit of man is often cast down, for while feeling that he has within him infinite capacities for acquiring knowledge, and attaining noble things, the limitations of time, and the hindering circumstances of his natural life, stay his onward march, fetter his hands, and put a drag on his loftiest imaginations and aspirations. As St. Paul says, he does but 'see through a glass darkly.' And the man who knows himself feels that it is best for him, so long as he has to live in a mortal tabernacle, and fight against the powers of darkness, not to have the perfection of the unseen universe laid quite bare before him. If it were, how could he look upon the world which sin has defiled, and upon the lives of the majority of men and women, without loathing and despair taking the place of faith and good works?

As human, man falters, and often falls; he slips, his heart fails, clouds obscure his mind, the atmosphere around him is hazy, and he can scarcely see his way. Then it is that the divine part of his nature asserts its supremacy, and comes to his aid; and with the prayer on his lips:

> 'Lead, kindly Light, amid the encircling gloom,
>   Lead Thou me on,'

he perseveres; he knows that he is 'far from home,'

but he knows also that the narrow way of the Cross leads straight to the Golden City ; and he prays the more earnestly :

> 'Lead Thou me on.
> Keep Thou my feet ; I do not ask to see
> The distant scene ; one step enough for me.'

It may be that the 'one step' will lead the mind from Nature up to Nature's God ; or it may enable man to fix the eye of the soul upon God as He was in the beginning, when the Son was 'in the bosom of the Father,' before the 'Spirit moved upon the face of the waters,' and the decree went forth, 'Let there be light.' The eye involuntarily closes for a moment, and the whole man is bowed down with a sense of reverential awe, as he realizes that a created being can be drawn so near to the Eternal as to be able to concentrate thought upon Him, 'whom no man hath seen or can see,' save only the God-man, who has declared Him and manifested Him unto the world. God has said : 'I dwell in the high and holy place, with him also that is of a contrite and humble spirit, to revive the spirit of the humble, and to revive the heart of the contrite ones.' When, in the 'fulness of time,' the Hypostatic Union of God and man was consummated, and the 'Light that lighteth every man coming into the world' was manifested in the person of Jesus Christ, great boldness of access was given to man ; now he soars like the eagle, and from resting on the Saviour's breast, he ascends in spirit; stands before the throne of the Alpha and Omega, and hears again the old and familiar words, 'Fear not.' Now, as in earlier days, the man whose soul is divinely illuminated penetrates to the presence-chamber of God, and there learns to know Him better, and to love Him more.

Great indeed is the 'Mystery of Godliness.' The more lowly-minded a man becomes, the more is he exalted; and as he repeats the words of saints and prophets, 'Holy, Holy, Holy, is the Lord of Hosts: the whole earth is full of His glory: Holy, Holy, Holy, Lord God Almighty, which was, and is, and is to come,' he is not utterly cast down; even in the depths of his humility he can contemplate the ever-blessed Trinity; for the Third Person of the Triune God has taught him that the high and lofty One is not far from him, and that the Second Person of the Trinity has effected an indissoluble union between him and his Maker. In that presence-chamber he learns that God is Truth, steadfast and unchangeable; and He has said that man shall one day 'know even as he is known.' In that day each immortal soul will see that from the grand centre, glowing with the fire of love, the rays of truth fell on men's minds and hearts as the Ruler of all judged best, fitting them to do their appointed work in the world. Just as certainly as a ray of light is decomposed into seven primary colours, when it is refracted through a prism, so each phase of truth, partially apprehended though it may be by man, will, under the teaching of the Holy Spirit, become re-moulded and fitted in with other truths, so that the whole truth will shine forth and appear, even in this life, to him who seeks for truth with a single eye and pure heart, one perfect whole, one light-giving centre. That centre is the Holy Trinity, the Father, the Son, and the Holy Ghost, one God in Trinity, and Trinity in Unity; 'the Father made of none, neither created nor begotten: the Son of the Father alone, not made, nor created, but begotten: the Holy Ghost of the Father and of the Son, neither made, nor created, nor begotten, but proceeding: and in this Trinity none is afore, or after another: none is greater or less than another; but the whole three persons are co-eternal together, and co-equal.' There is none like unto this Lord God Almighty, who 'clothes Himself with light as with a garment,' and 'dwelleth in the light which no man can approach unto.'

Creation declares God to be omnipotent, and lest the people whom He had chosen out of the nations to be witnesses for Him, and to whom He had said, 'Thou shalt worship the Lord thy God, and Him only shalt thou serve,' should forget the Creator when contemplating creation, and rob God of His glory when regarding the glories around them, He warned them to 'take heed,' lest, when they lifted up their eyes to heaven, and gazed upon the sun and moon and stars, and on all the hosts of heaven, they should be driven to worship them. 'I will not give my glory to another,' saith the Lord. 'God is a Spirit.' Of that Spirit He has imparted unto man, and 'in spirit and in truth' man must worship Him. It is derogatory to man to worship any created thing, for God has said to him, 'Look unto Me, and be ye saved, all the ends of the earth; for I am God, and there is none else. I have sworn by Myself; the word is gone out of My mouth in righteousness, and shall not return, that unto Me every knee shall bow, every tongue shall swear.' 'For thy Maker is thine husband; the Lord of hosts is His name; and thy Redeemer the Holy One of Israel; the God of the whole earth shall He be called.' Before this great and mighty God, the man who realizes his birthright privileges, and his wonderful tripartite nature, will not, if true to himself, be content with less than worshipping God with his whole being. He cannot cast a crown at the feet of the King of Kings, as St. John saw the elders in heaven cast their crowns before the throne, when they worshipped Him who sat on the throne, for man is not yet crowned; but when he would lift up his heart in prayer, he can, and he ought, to fall down upon his knees before the mercy-seat.

He cannot with his bodily eye see the Son of Man in glory, as St. John did, when he fell at His feet as one dead ; but he can and ought to prostrate his whole being before the hidden God of the Eucharist; for there, on the altars of His Church on earth, the Son of Mary is, under the forms of bread and wine. 'This is the bread which cometh down from heaven, that a man may eat thereof, and not die. I am the living bread which came down from heaven : if any man eat of this bread, he shall live for ever : and the bread that I will give is My flesh, which I will give for the life of the world. Verily, verily, I say unto you, Except ye eat the flesh of the Son of Man, and drink His blood, ye have no life in you. Whoso eateth My flesh, and drinketh My blood, hath eternal life ; and I will raise him up at the last day. For My flesh is meat indeed, and My blood is drink indeed. He that eateth My flesh, and drinketh My blood, dwelleth in Me and I in him. As the living Father hath sent Me, and I live by the Father; so he that eateth Me, even he shall live by Me.' 'Hath He said, and shall He not do it?' 'Lo, I am with you alway, even unto the end of the world,' was the Saviour's promise to the early Church, and all true and faithful members of His body believe that though heaven and earth may pass away, His words shall not pass away.

Few thinkers will deny that there is something

within them which is distinct from the evidences in Nature that are apprehended by the senses. This inward witness tells that God is, and, indeed, must be. What is this inward witness? It is no part of our material being. The natural body is but its environment. It is God's Spirit within man, testifying to the union of God and Man, and of the reality of the unseen. The recognition of this fact naturally leads to the exercise of the human intellect in the study of Nature; and in it, all who allow the higher part of their nature to guide them, find not only proofs of the existence of God, but revelations of His omnipotence, omniscience, and omnipresence. Science is but the unfolder and expounder of the attributes of Jehovah. When science has measured the distance which separates suns and planets; analyzed a flower or a crystal; or explained the nature of the laws which govern our world, what has science done save show man more clearly the Creator and Lawgiver who made all and orders all? The thing that is made proclaims its Maker; the laws of Nature declare a Lawgiver; but they cannot take His place. God within ourselves is our supreme Teacher. His still, small voice, which we call conscience—that mysterious power within us which directs and controls our apprehension of what is morally right—reveals the Creator as distinct from creation. It is this inward light, illuminating the ethical part of man's nature, which enables him to realize the darkness of evil, the power of that free-will which he possesses, and his consequent moral responsibility. Made in the image of God, he can discern between good and evil, and he knows that he has the power to choose between good and evil. Just as light causes us to apprehend what darkness is, so goodness demonstrates what evil is. Man, enlightened by the Holy Spirit, can know God apart from the teachings of material nature. He who chooses the good part, shrinks from evil, and yearns after that which is good. His own spirit enables him to form true conceptions of God's attributes, although those conceptions are at best but shadows of the great reality. Our first conception of God is that He is perfect. What, then, is perfection? It is that to which nothing can be added, and from which nothing can be subtracted. In a perfect being, the attributes of justice, mercy, and love must be co-equal, and not an atom must be allowed to preponderate in either so as to affect the perfect balance of the three. Omniscience holds the scales, hence the equal balance. When to omniscience we add omnipresence and omnipotence, and meditate upon the meaning of these words, reason enables us to apprehend the perfection of the Supreme Being, who permits us to address Him as 'Our Father.' We find ourselves, as it were, standing at the source of a great river. We see the water issuing from the earth, bubbling up from its unknown depths : we trace its course, and see it widening and deepening as it rolls on towards the ocean. At the meeting of the waters we lose sight of the river, but it is not lost; it has but united itself with the sea. The man who, while sailing down the stream of Time, contemplates the Divine Author of both spirit and matter, feels that he is gliding on towards the ocean of God's love, and that his spirit is returning to the God who gave it, to live for ever with angels, and archangels, and the 'spirits of just men made perfect' in the eternal spheres.

Once more, let us go back to the time when man was not, and learn, from what preceded his creation, the lesson that can also be learned from every page of the history of man. It is a lesson that each individual act of self-sacrifice illustrates, and each illustration proves the power that is exercised by spirit over matter, and testifies to the reality of the supernatural. The logic of facts suffices to prove that sacrifice is the offspring of love. Enthroned in sublime isolation, the Eternal Trinity held the first council. What was its subject? The creation of man. The Father, the Son and the Holy Ghost took counsel together ere man was made. Angels, principalities and powers were willed into existence; countless worlds were created; and when the foundations of the earth were laid, the 'morning stars sang together, and all the sons of God shouted for joy.' Why? When this world was to become a great battle-field, a great grave-yard, why should other worlds rejoice, and the angels sing? Only to the 'Three Persons in one God' could have been known Earth's history; but when its Corner-stone was laid, the sacrifice of the Son was virtually made, and the divine love in a sublime sacrifice filled all creation. This 'mystery of God' was hidden, until God's own time for revealing came; but, as it is written, 'before they call, I will answer,' so, before man was created or had fallen, the Saviour was ready, the Sacrifice for sin prepared, and the 'Gloria in Excelsis' was sung in heaven long before the angels were sent to sing it on earth. All was known to the Holy Trinity: man's disobedience in Eden; all the sin and all the suffering caused by sin; the outer and the inner life of each human being that should be born into the world, every thought, word and deed of each was known; all were seen in the light which proceeds from the Author of Light: and yet the creation of man was decreed.

We are not told that love is one of God's attributes, but that 'God *is* love'; and this helps us to understand how it is that laying the Corner-stone of what was to become a battle-field of woe was the cause of rejoicing throughout God's creation; for, in that world of strife, Love was to be sacrificed, in the

Person of Jesus Christ, in order that man might be restored to the image of God, and live for ever with Him. Christ took our flesh so that He might be like us in all things, sin excepted; and if we would be like Him in glory, we must be conformed to Him, and follow in His footprints through our valley of humiliation. He is the 'Way, the Truth and the Life.' From the cradle to the cross He lived the life of ordinary humanity; His divinity was veiled, but it was not hidden, save from those whom the 'God of this world had blinded.' Each of His disciples is a living sacrament, as He was, and still is, on earth, and all who are travelling along the road their Saviour trod, manifest in their works and conversation, in varying degrees, the same traits of character as those which the God-man manifested in perfection. Truth and equity in their dealings with their fellow-men; purity of life, charity towards those who are in need; courtesy and kindness to all; 'love, joy, peace, long-suffering, gentleness, goodness, faith, meekness, temperance,' distinguish them from those who live after the flesh; and those fruits of the Spirit prove their sonship, and their oneness with the Divine Son. They are manifestations of the divine, indwelling Spirit, and are no more of earth than the works of the flesh are of God. All Christian virtues are consummated in self-sacrifice, and in entire submission to the Divine Will. So it is that we learn of God, by the presence of His free Spirit within us, and we are led by the Spirit to study Nature and to find God everywhere.

> 'Thine, O Lord, is the kingdom,
>   Thine the glory and power;
> Thou hast kindled the starlight,
>   Thou hast moulded the flower.
>
> 'All things live by Thy presence,
>   All things obey Thy will;
> As the waters the ocean,
>   Earth Thy glory shall fill.
>
> 'Thou art the Father of spirits,
>   Thought is begotten of Thee;
> In Thine image begotten,
>   Glorious, boundless, and free.
>
> 'When its freedom transgressing,
>   Out of Thy ways hath strayed,
> Thou hast provided redemption,
>   Thou hast atonement made.
>
> 'Rolls this universe onward,
>   Circling the foot of Thy throne;
> Matter, and life, and spirit,
>   Guided by Thee alone.
>
> 'Righteous are all Thy judgments,
>   Perfect are all Thy ways.
> Who shall worthily serve Thee?
>   Who shall utter Thy praise?
>
> 'Therefore in peril and sorrow,
>   Therefore in joy's bright hour,
> Thine, O Lord, is the kingdom,
>   Thine the glory and power.'

Although God is everywhere present, man, from his temporary home on earth, instinctively raises his eyes to heaven when he prays to his Father, for in the highest heaven, wherever that may be, is the

THE GREAT SACRAMENT—GOD IN NATURE 61

throne of God, and there Jesus of Nazareth now is. When contemplating God in His works, one of man's first thoughts concerns the glory of the firmament! In the deep blue vault of space are the innumerable suns and planets which, in their ceaseless movements, are ever telling the story of Almighty power. The finite is lost in infinity as the fact is borne in upon the mind that this grand array of stellar worlds is only the outward and visible sign of the unseen reality, the material manifestation of the Creator. It is at such moments that the Great Sacrament is seen to be man's *ultima Thule*, as it is also his beginning. The magnitude of the stupendous whole impresses him when he reflects that this world is but a small body in the solar system. That system, consisting as it does of the sun with its attendant planets and asteroids, and the satellites of those planets, is but as a grain of sand upon the sea-shore, compared with the illimitable universe. Then, too, it is that he apprehends his own intellectual power, as it is shown in the invention of instruments which enable him to bring within his range of vision legions of stars which cannot be numbered; for when man has counted the 6,000 stars that are visible to the naked eye, the telescope will reveal to him myriads of other luminous orbs; and he will learn that the stars which we can see at night are really suns, each the centre of attraction for a whole galaxy of planets and satellites, which revolve around them.

The heaven-born genius that taught man how to make the telescope, has enabled him also to calculate the distance from the earth of those far-off worlds which have been thus revealed to him. Astronomers tell us that the distance between the earth and the sun is 38,000,000 leagues; that light travels 77,000 leagues in a second; therefore light from the sun takes seven minutes and thirteen seconds to reach the earth. Taking the distance between the earth and the sun as a standard of measurement, or unit, they compute the distance of one of the stars nearest to us to be 551,000 times our unit, and, supposing the light from this star in the constellation of the Swan to travel 77,000 leagues in a second, it would take nine and a half years to reach the earth. The polar star being distant from the earth 3,678,000 times that of the sun, the time occupied in the transit of light from that brilliant orb is fifty years: and when we consider that these and other splendid suns are the nearest to us, and are called stars of the first or second magnitude on account, not of their size, but of their brilliance, and then call to mind the fact that man can estimate the distance of telescopic stars of the fourteenth magnitude, whose light would take 100,000 years to reach the earth, we can account for man's power by believing what

THE GREAT SACRAMENT—GOD IN NATURE 63

revelation teaches, that we are made in the image of God; and, as His children, are endowed with a portion of His own spirit of wisdom and knowledge. He who made the eye limited its power of sight as, in His wisdom, He saw was best for man on the whole, but, as if to prove to the wise that the invisible is greater than the visible, and that spirit reigns over and controls matter, He endowed earnest seekers after truth with faculties which enable them to extend the power of sight, so as to bring within view 56 millions of suns; and astronomers only stop at that inconceivable number, because no telescope is powerful enough to enable them to see smaller stars than those of the fourteenth magnitude. Herschel, who examined the whole extent of what is called the Milky Way, estimated the number of stars in that vast nebula at 18,000,000. The length of the Milky Way has been estimated to be from 700 to 800 times the distance from Sirius to the sun, a distance which is 1,373,000 times that from the earth to the sun; so that a ray of light from a star at one extremity would take 15,000 years to reach one at the other extremity.

The mind is bewildered by thus dwelling upon what the telescope reveals. We see so far into the boundless depths of infinite space that we begin to understand what infinity means. We feel that we are 'fearfully and wonderfully made,' when the thought comes home to us, that the human intellect has enabled man to make an instrument which discloses wonders that overwhelm the imagination. He feels exultant, but his own greatness is an awe-inspiring fact to the Christian Philosopher, and his spirit bows down before the Giver of intellect in lowliest self-abasement and adoration. We know not yet what vaster fields for science to explore may be opened out to man; but we do know that, in the highest sense, his faculty is infinite; there is no limit to his attainments, even during the period of his mortal life. He may, and probably he will, go on soaring higher and higher, if only as he ascends he remembers his Creator, and keeps a firm hold of that chain which anchors him to the Rock of Ages. But if he let that slip from him, he will, notwithstanding all his great power, be but as a flashing meteor or a falling star. If man forgets God, and will believe in nothing higher than himself, then, however high-souled and lofty-minded he may be; to whatever height he may build up his knowledge, and however firmly he may fix each stone and set each jewel of his building by so-called facts and clear demonstrations, he, having no inherent self-sustaining power, will certainly fall like Lucifer at last, and have to learn concerning God in the bitter experiences of another stage of his existence.

Mighty as the power of God is seen to be in the

mystery of the million stars, we may gain a yet more exalted idea of His creative power by a study of the infinitely small. Each minute part of inanimate nature testifies to the skill and design of a Master-mind. The microscope demonstrates the perfection of infinitesimal particles up to that point where the microscope fails to disclose yet smaller things, as the telescope fails at a certain point to show us worlds beyond a measurable distance in space. 'Be still, and know that I am God,' is the voice of Revelation. All Creation echoes the words from height to height, and from depth to depth. Man's yearning to comprehend the incomprehensible cannot be satisfied in time. The ultimate of the microcosm as of the macrocosm is at present inconceivable. Man's investigations both of the seen and unseen universe can only end as they began, with God.

A geologist,[*] whose microscopic study of the rocks has made him eminent in that department of science, remarks, 'It is only recently that microscopical investigations have revealed the existence of extremely beautiful objects in many of the common rocks with which our country roads, and the streets of our towns, are paved and repaired. Black or dark gray stones of the most ordinary and unattractive appearance are found to be entirely composed of minute brilliant crystals whose

[*] S. Allport, Esq., F.G.S.

forms and colours correspond precisely with some of the larger specimens to be seen in our museums, or other collections of minerals. These microscopic crystals are, however, transparent, and exhibit far brighter colours than the corresponding larger and opaque specimens. The great beauty exhibited by a thin slice of one of these rocks is by no means confined to the minerals of which it is composed ; in fact, the structure of the rock, as seen in the way in which the constituents are arranged and grouped together, is as interesting and important as it is beautiful. In some rocks three or four different minerals are seen to be scattered irregularly throughout the mass ; in others two intercrystallized on a definite plan : or again, minute crystals of one kind only are grouped together in rosettes, or even aggregated in such a manner as to form the most striking resemblance to certain vegetable forms of growth. Doubtless the form of each individual crystal is determined by definite laws of crystallization, but the arrangement of vast numbers of these minute bodies in the well-defined symmetrical groups just mentioned still remains an unsolved problem.'

There is not, perhaps, in the whole range of science a branch that more emphatically proclaims the existence of a Lawgiver than crystallography does. Even a superficial knowledge of the crystalline relations of forms, and the classification of crystals, or the most cursory examination of the definite and symmetrical forms assigned to each, leads to the inevitable conclusion that they are moulded with mathematical precision, into the various forms peculiar to certain substances, by unvarying laws. A spirit of philosophical paganism may be satisfied that the working of unchanging laws through unknown ages is the outcome of fortuitous combinations, but the unbiased mind of man recognises that laws are not, and cannot be, self-executive, and that the existence of orderly laws of nature proves the thought and the will of a Lawmaker. To write even an elementary epitome of any branch of science is not necessary in the attempt which is here made to prove the reality of the supernatural. The present purpose is to demonstrate to those who have not, in these days of fierce competition for the means of existence, time to study and to think for themselves, that the material world is but the casket which holds the real crown of creation; the mortal body does but form an environment for the immortal soul. The vital energy, which some men substitute for God, is but the result of the active volition of the Almighty.

A few illustrations may, however, be given of the evident design, and the geometrical precision, which are to be met with in the crystal world.

When looking over a collection of crystals, the

first impression would come from their brilliance and beauty; the next feeling would be one of wonder at the great variety of the forms; these, however, according to the classification adopted by mineralogists, may be arranged in six well-defined systems. The primary forms of all known crystals are few, but the secondary ascertained forms of crystals are so numerous that no limit can be assigned to them. In one of the minerals, carbonate of lime, they amount to many hundreds; and mineralogists assert that 'thousands, and tens of thousands, more might occur under the operation of known and definite laws, so that all the alterations of figure which any given primary form can undergo might be determined *à priori*, if the extreme limits of the relative proportions of the edges considered to be cut off in producing new planes were known. Within well-ascertained limits, however, many thousands of possible secondary forms, belonging to each kind of primary, might be determined with absolute precision. The exact relations among primary and secondary forms may be determined mathematically, sometimes from measurement, and sometimes from parallelisms between certain edges of the secondary figures; and the mathematical processes may be either those of plane trigonometry, as applied by Haüy, or spherical trigonometry, as used by other authors; or analytical geometry, as applied by Professor

Whewell in a paper in the 'Phil. Trans.' for 1825 ; or by referring the planes of the crystal to the surface of a sphere, and denoting their positions stereographically, as shown in a paper by Professor Miller, of Cambridge, in the *London and Edinburgh Phil. Mag.* of February, 1835.'

These quotations on the formation of crystals, proving as they do the continuous working of an invariable law in the production of certain figures, are interesting even if the mind pursue the subject no further; but when the extreme slowness of natural crystallization is considered in connection with the construction of early crystalline rocks; when geologists point to the marvellously beautiful crystallized minerals embedded long ages ago in rocks that were ancient in prehistoric time ; when we fix the mind's eye upon the grand range of basaltic columns, known as the 'Giants' Causeway,' or stand in imagination in 'Fingal's Cave,' thought takes a wider and a higher flight, back into the unknown past, forward into the unknown future ; and the man of science who believes that the God of the universe is His own eternal Father, made strong by that belief, is in the attitude of the commander of an impregnable fortress ; his armour is proof against any weapon that can assail it ; he has a fountain of living water within his citadel which never fails, for its source is the same as that of the 'pure river of water of life, clear as crystal,' which St. John saw 'proceeding out of the throne of God and of the Lamb'; and he is able to hold his own against a host of unbelievers: 'his place of defence shall be the munitions of rocks; bread shall be given him, his water shall be sure.' Therefore he takes his stand in the present age of advanced knowledge and atheistic tendency, with firm, unwavering faith, assured that the laws which the crystal has taught him were governing Nature in the beginning and are everlasting laws, framed to keep in order the works of God while time and being last. There can be no alteration in perfect laws which, since they were made for a universe that is composed of spirit and matter, must work harmoniously, and be efficient for the purpose for which they are designed. Certain as we are from actual observation that the invisible sustains and controls the visible, we know but little in comparison with what we shall know; for as Carlyle has said, ' All visible things are emblems. What thou seest is not there on its own account; strictly speaking is not there at all. Matter exists spiritually, and to represent some idea, and body it forth.' It is so with human speech; words are not our thoughts, and oftener than not they fail to embody our thoughts. And what are our thoughts? Whence do they come? Do they originate themselves? We must wait before we can hope to understand fully; but Christ has given us light on this deep subject. 'Yet a little while and ye shall know that I am in My Father, and ye in Me, and I in you.' On these words we can rest, for they tell us that 'of Him, and through Him, and to Him, are all things': and that man's home is his Father's house, where he will learn lessons that cannot be mastered here below, and understand mysteries which, with his present opportunities of acquiring knowledge, are quite beyond his grasp.

The Giants' Causeway, to which reference has been made, is a striking illustration of the orderly arrangements of Nature. The compact texture of the basalt is a feature of the rock which is chiefly interesting on account of its columnar structure. The columns range in height from twenty to thirty feet, and form colonnades for a distance of nearly three miles. Some of these columns are pentagonal, others are three, four and six sided; each column is distinct from its neighbour, yet they are so close together that it is difficult to insert a knife between them. The most commanding series of columns, stretching out into the sea, is from twenty to forty feet broad. There they stand, like sentinels at their post, forming a grand breastwork, against which the wild waves of the ocean in the successive storms of the ages have dashed in vain. The ebb and flow of the tides have washed some of the columns from their original position, but the stupendous mass—which was believed in far-off days to be the work of a race of giants that had once inhabited the island—still remains. Travellers tell us that the most magnificent instance of basaltic formation occurs in the Oregon country, where the Columbia flows through the Rocky Mountains. There the explorer may see walls presenting 'successive rows of greenstone and basaltic columns, superimposed upon each other, divided by narrow horizontal beds of different composition,' towering above him from four hundred to one thousand feet in height.

We now direct attention to specimens of the crystal kingdom which are found in deep caverns.* In those dark places, where no ray of sunlight can find entrance, are the most wonderful varieties of crystals and stalactites. The hidden recesses of a range of mountain limestone have their arched roofs decorated with glistening pendants, and their walls covered with brilliant crystals, some pure transparent white, others tinted with bright and beautiful colours. There, too, may be seen huge

* These caverns, which occur in many limestone districts, have been formed by the long-continued percolation of surface water, which, by dissolving and removing portions of the carbonate of lime, has gradually produced underground channels and caverns; and during the lapse of ages the stalactites and groups of crystals, which now adorn the walls and sides of the cavities, have been slowly formed by the crystallization of the substances held in solution. The greater part of the beautiful minerals found in veins and cavities have crystallized out from various solutions, and have, therefore, quite a different origin from those found in igneous rocks.

THE GREAT SACRAMENT—GOD IN NATURE 73

stalactites, forming pillars which are perfect from floor to roof; here and there is a screen, adorned with Gothic tracery, or a pendant curtain, almost transparent, and falling in natural folds. No words can give more than a faint idea of the beauty of these caverns; and then, what a history each crystal has! What was it before it took a solid form? We are told that darkness was upon the face of the deep before the 'Spirit of God moved upon the face of the waters'; that the decree went forth, ' Let the waters under the heaven be gathered together unto one place, and let the dry land appear, and it was so'; that on the fourth day, God made two great lights; the greater light to rule the day, and the lesser light to rule the night.' When the time came that the Lord God caused it to rain upon the earth, the sunbeams did their beneficent work, drawing up countless drops from the ocean, dew-drops from the moistened earth, and rain-drops from the green things and flowers into the higher realm of creation, where they expanded and became ethereal, roaming through space with the winds, and helping to build up clouds which the sun could fringe with crimson and gold. Floating in the air, flecking the earth with their shadows, they waited until Nature's laws caused them again to fall in gentle rain, or in glittering morsels of ice, or feathery snow; some, perhaps, to be drawn up and etherealized by the sunbeams, some to trickle down the mountain-side into narrow crevices, passing through beds of limestone and other minerals until they reached their final destination and were transformed into crystals, causing the dark mountain caves to become 'things of beauty,' which should declare to man the unchanging nature of the laws that govern matter.

From the mountain cave let us descend to one of the deep sea valleys of ancient time, for there an unattractive-looking piece of stone leads us. It was broken off a larger piece, and left by the stone-breaker on his heap. It is a portion of the fossilized remains of the orthoceratite, a member of an extinct family of cephalopodous mollusca. This is embedded in the stone. The orthoceratite lived in a many-chambered dwelling, each chamber being skilfully walled in after the little animal had left it to build a larger one; and so the structure grew, until its inhabitant had attained its full size. Who gave the architect the skill to build, and the material of which to fashion a well-nigh imperishable dwelling-place? The orthoceratite died beneath the deep waters; its work remained, and one day a delicate, fragile creature, named lingula, and considered by geologists to belong to a class of animals named brachiopoda, saw that the work of the orthoceratite was a foundation on which it could fix itself securely by means of the fibrogelatinous peduncle depending from the extremity of the elongated bivalve shell in which it lived, and it elected to stay there. Gently moving to and fro by means of its slender pedicle in the still, deep waters which no tidal waves disturbed, the lingula lived its little life. Meanwhile other creatures of the sea, of delicate, plant-like appearance, and so low in the scale of animal creation that the naturalists of earlier days believed them to belong to the vegetable kingdom, commenced their work. These are known as anthozoa or zoophites. Myriads of them began to build, and soon they raised a wall of coral around the lingula, their foundation being the compact, hard work of the orthoceratite. The finished work of these three creatures of an ancient sea has been preserved in Nature's treasure-house, and illustrates one of the pages of her great book; each part is as perfect as when the architects built their own dwelling-places according to the design of the Master-builder. Time rolled on, and when the mighty forces upheaved the mountains, the oceanic valleys in which the orthocera lived became dry land; the strata below the old red system revealed to man the existence of this long-extinct family, which naturalists connect on one side with nautilidæ and on the other with ammonitidæ. Of these latter 'twin creatures of the sea,' a philosopher-poet has written:

'The Nautilus and the Ammonite
   Were launched in friendly strife,
Each sent to float in its tiny boat
   On the wide, wide sea of life.

' For each could swim on the ocean's brim,
   And when wearied its sails could furl,
And sink to sleep in the great sea-deep,
   In its palace, all of pearl.

' And theirs was a bliss more fair than this
   That we feel in our colder time ;
For they were rife in a tropic life,
   In a brighter and better clime.

' They swam 'mid isles, whose summer smiles
   No wintry winds annoy ;
Whose groves are palm, whose air is balm,
   Where life is only joy.

' They sailed all day through creek and bay
   And traversed the ocean deep,
And at night they sank on a coral bank,
   In its fairy bowers to sleep.

' And the monsters vast, of ages past,
   They beheld in their ocean caves ;
They saw them ride in their power and pride,
   And sink in their deep-sea graves.

' And hand in hand, from strand to strand,
   They sailed in mirth and glee—
Those fairy shells with their crystal cells,
   Twin creatures of the sea.

' And they came at last to a sea long past,
   But as they reached its shore,
The Almighty's breath spoke out in death,
   And the Ammonite lived no more.

' And the Nautilus now, in its shelly prow,
   As over the deep it strays,
Still seems to seek in bay and creek
   Its companion of other days.

> 'And thus do we on life's stormy sea,
>   As we roam from shore to shore,
> While tempest-tossed, seek the loved, the lost,
>   But find them on earth no more.
>
> 'Yet the hope, how sweet! again to meet,
>   As we look to a distant strand,
> Where heart finds heart, and no more they part,
>   Who meet in that better land.'*

It is difficult to condense even a part of the interesting information that geologists have made known about the nautilus and the ammonite; but brief extracts from their essays may be given, which will teach the same lesson that the crystal taught, although the one has to do with inanimate matter, the other with sentient life. We may notice in passing some remarks of Aristotle, who, after describing the naked cephalopods, says: 'There are also two polypi in shells; one is called by some nautilus, by others nauticus. It is like the polypus, but its shell resembles a hollow comb or pecten, and is not attached. The polypus ordinarily feeds near the seashore; sometimes it is thrown by the waves on the dry land, and the shell falling from it, is caught, and there dies. The other is in a shell like a snail, and this does not go out of its shell, but remains in it like a snail, and sometimes stretches forth its cirrhi externally.' The latter was, no doubt, the true nautilus; the former the beautiful argonauta, or paper nautilus, as it is com-

* Dr. Ick.

monly called. The shell is spiral, involute, membranaceous, and without chambers; it serves the creature that inhabits it for a boat, the membrane of which he can extend at pleasure, using it as a sail; his tentacula he uses as oàrs. Thus equipped, his fairy boat, light as a feather and white as snow, floats on the surface of calm waters, or, on the approach of danger, or when a storm arises, by absorbing a quantity of sea-water, he descends to his native dwelling-place, the bed of the ocean. The pearly nautilus has the same kind of tentacula and membranaceous sail, and in its habits it resembles the argonauta, but in the construction of its shell there is an essential difference: that of the argonauta is unilocular; that of the pearly nautilus is many-chambered; the divisions are concave towards the side next to the aperture, being perforated and connected by a syphon formed of a thin, testaceous matter, lined with a membrane of the animal. It has been well said of the shell of the nautilus: 'It is a vessel which no human hand has formed, guided by no human skill—a striking proof, amid the terrors and wonders of the deep, that, whilst nothing is too great for the controlling power of Omnipotence, nothing is too humble for His protecting care.'*

Of the origin of the fossil ammonite many a

* A most interesting account of this animal has been given by Professor Owen in his 'Memoir of the Pearly Nautilus.'

fabulous story has been invented in earlier days. One old legend tells of the snakes that infested the convent of Whitby, and says that, at the prayer of the saintly abbess, they were converted into stone, or, in Scott's words,

> 'How, of a thousand snakes, each one
> Was changed into a coil of stone,
>   When holy Hilda prayed.'

But science has relegated all these old stories to the region of fiction, and proved how nearly allied the ammonite was to the nautilus. In Dr. Buckland's 'Bridgwater Treatise' is described the various arrangements which secure lightness and strength to the shell, proving that no more perfect instrument for affording resistance to external pressure could be conceived. The Professor's summary is: 'As the animal increased in bulk, and advanced along the outer chamber of the shell, the spaces left behind it were successively converted into air-chambers, simultaneously increasing the power of the float. This float being regulated by a pipe passing through the whole series of the chambers, formed a hydraulic instrument of extraordinary delicacy, by which the animal could at pleasure control its ascent to the surface or descent to the bottom of the sea. To creatures that sometimes floated, a thick and heavy shell would have been inapplicable; and as a thin shell inclosing air would be exposed to various and often intense degrees of pressure at the bottom, we find a series of provisions to afford resistance to such pressure in the mechanical construction both of the external shell, and of the internal transverse plates which formed the air-chambers. First, the shell is made up of a tube coiled round itself, and externally convex. Secondly, it is fortified by a series of ribs and vaultings disposed in the form of arches and domes on the convex surface of this tube, and still further adding to its strength. Thirdly, the transverse plates that form the air-chambers supply also a continuous succession of supports, extending their ramifications, with many mechanical advantages, beneath those portions of the shell which, being weakest, were most in need of them.' Who can read this description and fail to see direct and conclusive evidence of an omniscient and omnipotent Designer, who has been actively engaged in the arrangement of every atom that composed these beautiful creatures? The Ammonite is a perfect embodiment of the will of One, who, perfect Himself, could not will the creation of anything imperfect, and, as such, unfitted to fulfil the purpose for which it was created.

If the fact were not proved beyond the possibility of doubt, that men of great intellectual power and acute observation do deny the existence of God, and openly avow their unbelief, the mass of mankind would not believe it to be possible that such a paradox as cultured reason and unbelief in a Giver of reason could live in the minds of men. Laplace, after observing that 'the curve described by a single molecule of air, or any fluid, is subjected to laws as certain as those of the planetary orbits,' adds, 'there is no difference between them, but what arises from our own ignorance.' Unbelief can only be the child of ignorance—that is, ignorance of fundamental truth; and we cannot doubt that the knowledge which now usurps the place of reason will one day crown itself by acknowledging its lawful Sovereign.

To the notes on the nautilus and the ammonite, it will be well to add Dr. Buckland's concluding observations upon the affinities of the chambered shells of Cephalopods. He writes: 'It results from the view we have taken of the zoological affinities between living and extinct species of chambered shells, that they are all connected by one plan of organization, each forming a link in the common chain which unites existing species with those that prevailed among the earliest conditions of life upon our globe; and all attesting the identity of the design that has effected so many similar ends through such a variety of instruments, the principle of whose construction is in every species fundamentally the same. Throughout the various living and extinct genera of chambered shells, the use of the air-chambers and syphons, to adjust the specific gravity of the animals in rising and sinking, appears to have been identical. The addition of a new transverse plate within the conical shell added a new air-chamber, larger than the preceding one, to counterbalance the increase of weight that attended the growth of the shell and body of these animals. These beautiful arrangements are, and ever have been, subservient to a common object, namely, the construction of hydraulic instruments of essential importance in the economy of creatures destined to move sometimes at the bottom and at other times upon or near the surface of the sea. The delicate adjustments whereby the same principle is extended through so many grades and modifications of a single type show the uniform and constant agency of some controlling Intelligence : and in searching for the origin of so much method and regularity amidst variety, the mind can only rest when it has passed back through the subordinate series of second causes to that great first cause, which is found in the will and power of a common Creator.'

We now direct the attention of the reader to the coral insect and its work. One becomes almost lost in thought when regarding the tiny polyps that are still at work beneath the waters, adding to the formations of ages, working by the same law, and taught by the same Teacher as their progenitors.

THE GREAT SACRAMENT—GOD IN NATURE 83

Their work is one of the wonders of the world. Each little builder lives and dies at his post. His work being finished, he rests from his labour, and another builds on the foundation he has laid: and when man goes back into the past, and investigates the work of the early Cyathophylloids in Paleozoic time, and then visits the coral islands and reefs that are now being raised above the waters, stretching for hundreds of miles along the shores of continents, his pride in his material work must be brought low. Man built great Babylon, and Rome, and Heliopolis; man raised the Pyramids, and set the massive stones of Baalbec in their places; but what are these achievements when compared with those of the coral insect?

In order to give those who have not studied geology, and other natural sciences, some idea of the time during which these architects of the ocean have been working, it will be well to give the following summary of geological time from the interesting work on 'Corals and Coral Islands,' by James D. Dana, LL.D. 'Geological history begins with what has been called *Azoic* time, *Azoic* signifying the absence of life. But the rocks supposed to be *Azoic* have been found to afford evidence of the existence of the simplest kinds of life during their formation; and the era they represent is, therefore, more correctly styled the *Archeozoic*, from the Greek for *beginning* and *life*.'

The other grand subdivisions of geological time are as follows :

1. Paleozoic time (named from the Greek for *ancient life*), in the course of which the earliest corals, mollusks, crustaceans, insects, fishes and reptiles existed. It includes three ages: (1) the *Silurian;* (2) the *Devonian*, or age of fishes ; and (3) the *Carboniferous*, or age of coal-plants, when the most extensive beds of mineral coal of the world were originated.

2. Mesozoic time, or that of *mediæval life*. It corresponds to the age of reptiles—being the era, not of the earliest reptiles, but that of their climax in number, size, and variety. This age is divided into three periods : first, or earliest, the Triassic ; second, the Jurassic, to which the Oolitic era belongs ; and third, the Cretaceous, or that of the chalk.

3. Cenozoic time, or that of *recent life*, as the term signifies. It is modern in the aspect of its species, compared with the Mesozoic, and still more so compared with the Paleozoic. The highest and dominant species were mammals.

Then came the creation of man in God's image. These geological facts, clearly demonstrated by the earth's crust, irresistibly lead the mind, as the calculations of astronomers also do, to dwell upon infinity. The latter proclaim that space is illimitable ; the former, that the ages man can count are

THE GREAT SACRAMENT—GOD IN NATURE 85

but the moments of eternity. The slowness of the formation of coral islands and reefs deserves attention, and this we will introduce with Dr. Dana's explanations of the formation of coral.

'Science, while it penetrates deeply the system of things about us, sees everywhere, in the dim limits of vision, the word "mystery." Surely there is no reason why the simplest of organisms should bear the impress most strongly. If we are astonished that so great deeds should proceed from the little and low, it is because we fail to appreciate that little things, even the least of living or physical existences in nature, are, under God, expressions throughout of comprehensive laws, laws that govern alike the small and the great. It is not more surprising, nor a matter of more difficult comprehension, that a polyp should form structures of stone (carbonate of lime) called coral, than that the quadruped should form its bones, or the mollusk its shell. The processes are similar, and so is the result. In each case it is a simple animal secretion—a secretion of stony matter from the aliment which the animal receives, produced by the parts of the animal fitted for this secreting process; and in each case carbonate of lime is a constituent, or one of the constituents, of the secretion. This power of secretion is, then, one of the *first* and most common of those that belong to living tissues; and though differing in different organs according to their end or function, it is all one process, both in its nature and cause, whether in the animalcule or in man. It belongs eminently to the lowest kinds of life. These are the best stone-makers; for in their simplicity of structure they may be almost all stone, and still carry on the processes of nutrition and growth. Throughout geological time they were the agents appointed to produce the material of limestones, and also to make even the flint, and many of the siliceous deposits of the earth's formations. Coral is never, therefore, the *handiwork* of the many-armed polyps; for it is no more a result of labour than bone-making in ourselves. And, again, it is not a collection of cells into which the coral animals may withdraw for concealment any more than the skeleton of a dog is its house or cell; for every part of the coral—or corallum, as it is now called in science—of a polyp, in most reef-making species, is enclosed within the polyp, where it was formed by the secreting process.

'Coral is made by organisms of four very different kinds. These are: 1. Polyps, the most important of coral-making animals, the principal source of the coral reefs of the world.

'2. Animals related to the little hydra of fresh waters, and called Hydroids (a division under the Acalephs), which Agassiz has shown form the very common and often large corals called millepores.

'3. The lowest tribe of molluscs, called Bryozoans,

THE GREAT SACRAMENT—GOD IN NATURE 87

which produce delicate corals, sometimes branching and moss-like (whence the name, from the Greek for *moss-animal*), and at other times in broad plates, thick masses, and thin incrustations. Although of small importance as reef-makers at the present time, in a former age of the world—the Paleozoic—they so abounded over the sea bottom that some beds of limestone are half-composed of them.

'4. Algæ or sea-weeds, some kinds of which would hardly be distinguished from corals, except that they have no cells or pores.'

' A good idea of a polyp may be had from comparison with the garden aster; for the likeness to many of them in external form, as well as delicacy of colouring, is singularly close. The aster consists of a tinted disc bordered with one or more series of petals. And, in exact analogy, the polyp-flower, in its most common form, has a disc fringed around with petal-like organs called tentacles. Below the disc, in contrast with the slender pedicel in the ordinary plant, there is a stout cylindrical pedicel or body, often as broad as the disc itself, and sometimes not much longer, which contains the stomach and internal cavity of the polyp; and the mouth, which opens into the stomach, is at the centre of the disc. Here then the flower-animal and the garden-flower diverge in character, the difference being required by the different modes of nutrition, and other characteristics in the two kingdoms of Nature. The coral polyp is as much an animal as a cat or a dog.

'The prominent subdivisions of polyps here recognised are :

'(i.) *Actinoid Polyps.*—Related to the actinia, or sea-anemone, in tentacles and interior structure, and having, as in them, the number of tentacles and interior septa a multiple of six. The name *Actinia* is from the Greek for *ray*.

'(ii.) *Cyathophylloid Polyps.*—Like the Actinoids in tentacles and interior structure, except that the number of tentacles and interior septa is a multiple of four.

" (iii.) *Alcyonoid Polyps.*—Having eight fringed tentacles, and other characters mentioned beyond ; as the Gorgoniæ, and Alcyonia.'

Beautiful beyond the power of the mind to conceive, or of words to describe, are these creatures of the deep, and the architecture of some of them surpasses themselves in beauty. With bodies of brilliant colours which, in some species, are so transparent that the organism can be seen through the delicate texture of the outer envelope, they live and work beneath the waters. Nature's economist here puts the question, Why all this beauty, when there were no eyes to enjoy it? But beauty exists because, ' In the beginning . . . the Spirit of God

THE GREAT SACRAMENT—GOD IN NATURE

moved upon the face of the waters;' and man finds delight therein, inasmuch as he bears the image of his Maker.

'The Alcynoids,' Dr. Dana says, 'include some of the gayest and most delicate of coral shrubs. Almost all are flexible, and wave with the motion of the water. They contribute but little to the material of coral reefs, but add largely to the beauties of the coral landscape. Not only are the polyps of handsome tints, but the whole shrub is usually of a brilliant orange, yellow, scarlet, crimson, or purple shade. Dun colours also occur, as ash-gray, and dark brown, and almost black. Some kinds, the Spongiadiæ, are too flexible to stand erect, and they hang from the coral ledges, or in the coral caves, in gorgeous clusters of scarlet, yellow, and crimson colours.

'The Actiniæ vary immensely in size, from the eighth of an inch and smaller in the diameter of the disc to over a foot—though commonly between half an inch and three inches. One species, from the Panmotu Coral Archipelago in the Pacific, had a diameter across its disc of fourteen inches; and it was also one of the most beautiful in those seas, having multitudes of tentacles with carmine tips and yellowish bases, around the open centre, gathered into a number of large groups or lobes.

'With rare exceptions, Actiniæ live attached to stones, shells, or the sea bottom, or are buried at the base in the sand or mud. The attached species have the power of locomotion, through the muscles of the base, but only with extreme slowness. The loose stones on a sea-shore near low-tide level often have Actinia fixed to their under surface. A very few species swim or float at large in the ocean. These polyps have also the faculty of reproducing lost parts; and to such an extent that a mere fragment, if it be from the lower part, and include a portion of the base, will reproduce all the rest of the Actinia, even to the disc, tentacles, and stomach. Thus the mere forcible tearing of an Actinia from the rock to which it is attached may result in starting a crop of new Actiniæ.

'The general characters of the coral-making Actinoid Polyps are the same as in the Actiniæ. Their more striking peculiarities depend on the secretion of coral, making them fixed species, and involving an absence of the base; and, in the case of the majority of the species, on the extent to which they multiply by buds, in imitation of species in the vegetable kingdom.'

The extreme beauty and variety of the corallums of these polyps are known to all who study the wonders of the sea, but we proceed to notice the work of the Cyathophylloid Polyps. In it we find abundant proof of the truth of Professor Sedgwick's words, in his 'Studies of Cambridge.' 'The geologist counts his time, not by celestial cycles, but by an index he has found in the solid framework of the globe itself. He sees a long succession of monuments, each of which may have required a thousand ages for its elaboration. He arranges them in chronological order, observes in them the marks of skill and wisdom, and finds within them the tombs of the ancient inhabitants of the earth.'

St. John wrote—'In the beginning was the Word, and the Word was with God, and the Word was God. The same was in the beginning with God. All things were made by Him, and without Him was not anything made that was made. In Him was *life;* and the life was the light of man.' God is life, and life, without which there could be no inanimate matter, is God. The work of the coral insect teaches us this great truth; and man would do well to study Nature more than he does, and learn more from her teaching. The limestone rocks of past ages were reared by the secretions of living polyps; and what mighty monuments they are of the Great Sacrament, God in Nature ! The polyps are ' the best stone-makers.' They are the agents appointed by their Creator to produce the material of limestone; and the results of their working in perfect obedience to law are truly surprising. But man is the agent appointed to be lord of creation, to work consciously for the glory of his God; to train himself for the higher life to which he is destined; and to raise on earth 'living stones,' which are to be set in the eternal Temple of Truth. When we realize what man was when created; what he ought to be, nay, what he is, notwithstanding the degradations of sin; and when we look around upon the failure of man to reach his best, we almost reverence the little coral insect for its perfect fulfilment of its appointed work. We see, in the great antiquity of the coral world, in the continuity of the work of these builders, and in the strength and beauty of their work, one of the grandest, and, in its details, one of the most suggestive illustrations of the way in which Divine Power can work by the lowliest means which the material world affords.

We must go over the entire Pacific Ocean if we would form an adequate idea of the extent of the work of the polyps, for the reef-builders prefer warmer waters than those which surround the British Isles. 'An isothermal line crossing the ocean where the waters through the coldest winter month have a mean temperature not below 68° F., one north of the equator, and another south, bending in its course towards or from the equator wherever the marine currents change its position, will include all the growing reefs in the world; and this area of waters may be properly called the *coral-reef seas*.

'Through the *torrid* region, where the temperature of the surface is never below 74° F. for any month of the year, all the prominent genera of reef-forming species are abundantly represented. The Feegee seas afford magnificent examples of torrid-region productions.

'The rate of growth of coral is a subject but little understood. We do not refer here to the progress of a reef in formation, which is another question complicated by many co-operative causes; but simply to the rapidity with which particular living species increase in size. There is no doubt that the rate is different for different species. It is moreover probable that it corresponds with the rate of growth of other allied polyps that do not secrete lime. The rate of growth of Actiniæ might give us an approximation to the rate of growth in coral animals of like size and general character; for the additional function of secreting lime would not necessarily retard the maturing of the polyp; and from the rate of growth of the same animals in the young state, we might perhaps draw some inferences as to the rate in polyps of corresponding size. But no satisfactory observations on this point have yet been made.'*

After enumerating many distinct causes affecting in greater or lesser degree the growth of coral, and giving interesting details of careful observations which from time to time have been made, Dr. Dana remarks: 'Whatever the uncertainties, it is

* Dr. Dana published the second edition of his work on 'Corals' in 1875.

evident that a reef increases in height or extent with extreme slowness. If the rate of upward progress is one-sixteenth of an inch a year, it would take for the addition of a single foot to its height one hundred and ninety years, and for five feet a thousand years. Coral reefs and coral islands are structures of the same kind under somewhat different conditions. They are made in the same sea, by the same means; in fact, a coral island has in all cases been a coral reef through a large part of its history, and is so still over much of its area. The terms, however, are not synonymous. *Coral islands* are reefs that stand isolated in the ocean, away from other lands, whether now only raised to the water's edge and half submerged, or covered with vegetation; while the term *coral reefs*, although used for reefs of coral in general, is more especially applied to those which occur along the shores of high islands and continents.

'Coral reefs are banks of coral rock built upon the sea bottom about the shores of tropical lands. In the Pacific these lands, with the exception of New Caledonia and others of large size to the westward, are islands of volcanic or igneous rocks, and they often rise to mountain heights. The coral reefs which skirt their shores are ordinarily wholly submerged at high tide; but at the ebb they commonly present to view a broad, flat, bare surface of rock, just above the water-level, strongly contrasting with the steep slopes of the encircling island.

'Could we raise one of these coral-bound islands from the waves, we should find that the reefs stand upon the submarine slopes, like massive structures of artificial masonry; some forming a broad, flat platform or shelf ranging around the land, and others encircling it like vast ramparts, perhaps a hundred miles or more in circuit. The reefs that were near the water-line of the coast would be seen to have stood in the shallowest water, while the outer ramparts rested on the more deeply-submerged slopes. It is obvious that with a given slope to the declivity of the land, the thickness of the reef resting upon it may be directly determined, as it would be twice as great two hundred feet from the shore as at one hundred feet. The only difficulty, therefore, in correctly determining the depth or thickness of any given reef arises from the uncertainty with regard to the submarine slope of the land. It is, however, admitted, as the result of extensive observation, that in general these slopes correspond nearly with those of the land above water. Mr. Darwin has thus estimated the thickness of the reefs of the Gambier groups and some other Pacific islands, and he arrives at the conclusion, as his figures indicate, that some coral reefs at their outer limits are at least two thousand feet in thickness.

'Coral islands resemble the reefs, except that a

lake or lagoon is encircled instead of a mountainous island. A narrow rim of coral reef, generally but a few hundred yards wide, stretches around the enclosed waters. In some parts the reef is so low that the waves are still dashing over it into the lagoon; in others it is verdant with the rich foliage of the tropics. When first seen from the deck of a vessel, only a series of dark points is descried just above the horizon. Shortly after the points enlarge into the plumed tops of cocoa-nut trees, and a line of green, interrupted at intervals, is traced along the water's surface. Approaching still nearer, the lake and its belt of verdure are spread out before the eye, and a scene of more interest can scarcely be imagined. The surf, beating loud and heavy along the margin of the reef, presents a strange contrast to the prospect beyond—the white coral beach, the massy foliage of the grove, and the embosomed lake with its tiny islets. The colour of the lagoon water is often as blue as the ocean, although but ten or twenty fathoms deep; yet shades of green and yellow are intermingled, where patches of sand or coral-knolls are near the surface; and the green is a delicate apple shade, quite unlike the ordinary muddy tint of shallow waters.

'The belt of verdure, though sometimes continuous around the lagoon, is usually broken into islets separated by varying intervals of bare reef;

and through one or more of these intervals a ship-channel often exists, opening into the lagoon. The larger coral islands are thus a string of islets along a line of reef. These lagoon islands are called *atolls*, a word of Maldive origin. In the larger atolls the waters within look like the ocean, and are similarly roughened by the wind, though not to the same extent. The lagoon is in fact but a fragment of the ocean cut off by more or less perfect walls of coral reef-rock; and the reef is here and there surmounted by verdure, forming a series of islets.'

What are man's mightiest breakwaters compared with these coral reefs? Man, when building up his sea walls, has to wait for the ebb of the tide; and he has to protect himself in every possible way that skill and forethought can devise against the power of the unseen forces which are ever in motion. The polyps build their walls amid the waves of an ocean that is never at rest. Through long ages they toil on unseen until their work appears above the waters, and then those agents of Almighty power, the winds and the waves, deposit atoms of organic matter upon the upraised coral, and living things of grace and beauty spring up and grow beneath the skies of a tropical clime, and crown the work of the polyp with the green things of an earth on which the sunlight rests as a gloria, and warms and cherishes them until at last man comes and dwells beneath their shadow. These wonders of creation, ever growing and unfolding new beauties through the energy breathed into them by the Author of Life, are sufficient in themselves to prove to man that he, while on earth, is in his infancy. This planet is, first, his cradle; then his school, where he learns to read and to think; and his elementary lessons, if well-learned, enable him to do much for the good of his own and of succeeding generations, both from a material and social, and also from a scientific and ethical point of view. He builds cities, temples and palaces, which stand for centuries; but they crumble beneath the ravages of time, and become ruins. As ruins—time-worn and moss-grown—they stand through many succeeding centuries, often more beautiful than in their palmiest days, when they were as perfect as man could make them. But they crumble into dust at last. The natural man, however, closes his eyes alike to the teaching of Nature and to the results of his own labour, and so fails to learn the lesson that all around him is ceaselessly proclaiming—viz., that material things in their present condition were created only for *time*, but were set in perfect adaptation to the place they had to occupy; while man was made for *eternity*, and therefore, all his real greatness is to be found in another sphere—the sphere of the 'supernatural.'

THE GREAT SACRAMENT—GOD IN NATURE

The completed *atoll* is thus described by Dr. Dana : 'The atoll, a quiet scene of grove and lake, is admirably set off by the contrasting ocean. Its placid beauty rises to grandeur when the storm rages, and the waves foam and roar about the outer reefs ; for the child of the sea still rests quietly in unheeding and dreamy content. This coral-made land is firm, because it is literally *sea-born*, it having been built out of sea-products by the aid of the working ocean. And so with the groves : they were planted by the waves, and hence the species are those that can defy the encroaching waters, and meet the various conditions in which they are placed. The plants, therefore, take firm hold of the soil, and grow in all their natural strength and beauty. Only an occasional coral island has a completely encircling grove, and is hence a model atoll. But the many in which a series of green islets surround the lagoon are often but little less attractive, especially when the several islets present varied groupings of palms and other foliage.'

The torrid zone has been well-called a 'coral zone.' It is as a jewelled belt encircling the earth ; for many of its coral islands are gems of rare beauty. We have glanced at their surface ; their base lies many fathoms deep. It is well known that the bed of the vast Pacific Ocean testifies to periods of elevation and subsidence of the earth's crust in remote epochs, and of volcanic action on a gigantic scale. It was when the subterranean forces had exhausted their strength, and the fires of the volcanic peaks and mountains had become extinct, that a gradual subsidence caused the mountains to disappear below the waters, and then the polyps began to build their coral structures. Age after age, as the slowly progressing subsidence went on, countless generations continued the work, which in later days was to rise above the waters, and proclaim by its beauty and its power of resistance to the stormiest waves, 'The Hand that made us is Divine.' Dr. Dana gives an account of the geographical distribution of islands and reefs; of the changes in levels in coral regions, and of the subsidence in Pacific coral regions; and thus sums up this interesting part of his subject.

'The facts surveyed give us a long insight into the past, and exhibit to us the Pacific once scattered over with lofty lands, where now there are only humble monumental atolls. Had there been no growing coral, the whole would have passed without a record. These permanent registers exhibit in enduring characters some of the oscillations which the "stable" earth has since undergone.

'From the actual size of the coral reefs and islands, we know that the whole amount of high land lost to the Pacific by the subsidence was at the very least fifty thousand square miles. But since atolls are necessarily smaller than the land

THE GREAT SACRAMENT—GOD IN NATURE 101

they cover, and the more so the further subsidence has proceeded; since many lands, owing to their abrupt shores or to volcanic agency, must have had no reefs about them and have disappeared without a mark; and since others may have subsided too rapidly for the corals to retain themselves at the surface, it is obvious that this estimate is far below the truth. It is apparent that in many cases islands now disjoined have been once connected, and thus several atolls may have been made about the heights of a subsiding land of large size. Such facts show additional errors in the above estimate, evincing that the scattered atolls and reefs tell but a small part of the story.'

The foregoing notes of what has been gathered from a few pages of the 'Book of Nature' are but illustrative. A student must search the deeps, and soar into the heights, if he would read Nature's records aright. Science sincerely studied can never lead him astray, for the facts it reveals are but the material manifestations of the will of the Divine Maker. Theories that are based only upon what some man or men have observed may lead some scientific men to lose sight of God. But when they have moved into the shadow of a cloud that obscures the sun, what is there to take the place of that guiding Light which they have lost? Only the *ignis fatuus* that is kindled by their own limited knowledge of created things. That very knowledge, moreover, has been acquired by an ability which man alone of all earth-born creatures possesses; by a power which, if not given to him by the Creator, man cannot account for or explain; a power which is far above the laws which govern Nature, for it enables man to understand those laws, and even, to a great extent, to make them subservient to his will. Yet he rejects the Lawmaker, and follows his reason while denying the Giver of reason. But do what he will theoretically, man cannot get rid of two stern facts which are always confronting him: (1) The present life of man with all its concomitants; with its involuntary commencement, and its certain ending. (2) Consequent upon this fact, the purposelessness of man's life, if there be nothing beyond the shore of time—nothing but this material world. 'Ashes to ashes, dust to dust,' is the motto inscribed by the finger of God upon all that does not possess *life*—the life that knows no ending, because it is the breath of Him who is the fountain of life. 'Thou, Lord, in the beginning hath laid the foundation of the earth; and the heavens are the work of Thine hands. They shall perish, but Thou remainest; and they all shall wax old as doth a garment; and as a vesture shalt Thou fold them up, and they shall be changed: but Thou art the same, and Thy years shall not fail.'

Those who see in the fresh discoveries which science is ever making, further illustrations of the working of definite laws—which are in reality the agents of the active will and purposes of a higher Power—will see also in each new discovery an additional proof of the *necessary* existence of one Supreme Ruler, who *must* be all-wise and all-powerful. Moreover, those who have the strongest faith in God, the firmest grasp of his Almighty Hand, the deepest love for Him, not so much for what He has done for them, or in view of his glorious works, as for what He *is* in Himself, have the clearest perception of the fact, that all creation has been brought into existence and is sustained by *One like unto themselves.* With this difference, however,—the One is the central Sun of the Universe, and man but a ray of light emanating from the Sun.

One like unto themselves! Even so, because, although God is on His throne in the highest heaven, and man, at present, is leaning on His footstool, man can see more clearly day by day, in the material world and in the spiritual part of his own being, evidences of design; evidences of direction and control; evidences of fitness, correspondence, and harmony; evidences of adaptation and co-operation. And when man was made in the image of God, the attributes of God were bestowed upon him in such measure as the Father, in His infinite wisdom, saw was best; but the measure is to be increased until they shall 'come into the unity of the faith, and of the knowledge of the Son of God, unto a perfect man, unto the measure of the stature of the fulness of Christ.'

Such is man, and such is his destiny. If he were less than he is, he could not be the image of God; if his destiny were less exalted, he could not be one with the Son, and his body could not be the temple of the Holy Ghost: nor, unless he were all this, could he understand, even in part, and use to effect his own purpose, the laws which govern the seen and unseen universe. It is the union of matter and spirit, life connecting created things—in short, God incorporated in His works, which establishes what science will doubtless one day proclaim to be a scientific fact, namely, that the same laws govern the seen and the unseen. *Therefore* arises the value of all true knowledge acquired by man in the region of creation. All of truth that he gathers and lays by in store, is but the foundation on which he will build in the *next stage* of his existence; and when man is set free from his mortal environment he will find that all he has gathered here is his own for ever; and that he is working still on the old principles which have reached a higher sphere of operation; that the same laws were in force under altered conditions, and that he is just as much his same old self as when his body kept him in the lower sphere. So our most blessed Lord taught us, when He said to the penitent thief, 'To-day thou shalt be *with Me* in Paradise;' and afterwards, to His terrified disciples—who, when their eyes were opened so that they could discern what we call spiritual existences, saw Jesus standing in the midst of them, and were 'affrighted, and supposed that they had seen a spirit'—' Why are ye troubled? and why do thoughts arise in your hearts? Behold My hands and My feet, that it is Myself; handle me, and see; for a spirit hath not flesh and bones, as ye see Me have.'

Does he who believes that the holy Scriptures contain a revelation from God to man, and at the same time disbelieves and ridicules all that is commonly called 'supernatural,' ever bring reason to bear upon the fact that the words recorded were uttered by superhuman lips? He who spoke them had passed through closed doors, yet He was none the less Jesus of Nazareth. The disciples were not endowed with new senses in order to enable them to see what, a moment before, was to them invisible; to handle and feel what was intangible: but their senses became capable of discerning things not within range of their ordinary power of sight and touch. That was all. No law was broken, no new one made. That which man calls miraculous will perhaps, hereafter, be scientifically proved to be neither more nor less than evidence of the development, or unfolding, of the esoteric working of Almighty power. We have spoken of the senses of sight and touch; but there was yet another evidence which the risen Lord vouchsafed—that afforded by the sense of hearing, proving that it was He Himself, and not another, who was still among those who sought for Him and loved Him. The familiar voice, pronouncing the one word, 'Mary,' drew forth the exultant cry of 'Rabboni!'

A talented lecturer, eminent for his scientific attainments, has given a description of the common 'nettle,' as it appears when seen through a powerful microscope, and after stating that within its tiny hairs currents of a limpid liquid, containing innumerable and exceedingly minute granules, might be seen in a state of ceaseless activity, coursing swiftly in opposite directions within the twenty-thousandth part of an inch of one another, he remarks, 'Currents similar to those of the hairs of the nettle have been observed in a great multitude of different plants, and weighty authorities have suggested that they probably occur in more or less perfection in all young vegetable cells. If such be the case the wonderful noonday silence of a tropical forest is, after all, due only to the dulness of our hearing, and could our ears catch the murmur of these tiny maelstroms as they whirl in innumerable myriads of living cells which constitute each tree, we should be stunned as with the roar of a great city.'

Here again, in the silent solitude of a great forest, man, by the power of his own intellect, is convicted of incompleteness; the partially developed state of his senses is brought home to him; the mystery of life is manifest in that part of the 'Great Sacrament' which is encircling him. He sees that all the beauties of the vegetable kingdom are the result of obedience to law. The continuous working of law caused the trees to grow, and year by year it encircles their giant trunks with rings which enable men to tell their age: but what gave law its potent energy? Who framed it to give strength to the tree, whiteness to the lily, perfume to the rose, and to the lowly harebell its slender stem? No other than He who said, 'Consider the lilies of the field, how they grow; they toil not, neither do they spin: and yet I say unto you, that even Solomon in all his glory was not arrayed like one of these. Wherefore, if God so clothe the grass of the field, which to-day is, and to-morrow is cast into the oven, shall He not much more clothe you, O ye of little faith?'

The lily, growing in obedience to law, ever remains perfect, as when first fashioned by the Divine mind. Man, through disobedience to law, has lost his perfection, and Solomon's outward splendour, fashioned by men, cannot compare with that of the lily of the field. Nevertheless, what saith the Lord? 'Fear not; for thou shalt not be ashamed: neither be thou confounded; for thou shalt not be put to shame: for thou shalt forget the shame of thy youth, and shalt not remember the reproach of thy widowhood any more. For thy Maker is thine husband; the Lord of Hosts is His name; and thy Redeemer the Holy One of Israel; the God of the whole earth shall He be called. For the Lord hath called thee as a woman forsaken and grieved in spirit, and a wife of youth, when thou wast refused, saith thy God. For a small moment have I forsaken thee; but with great mercies will I gather thee. In a little wrath I hid My face from thee for a moment; but with everlasting kindness will I have mercy on thee, saith the Lord thy Redeemer.' 'Let not your heart be troubled: ye believe in God, believe also in Me. In My Father's house are many mansions: if it were not so, I would have told you. I go to prepare a place for you. And if I go and prepare a place for you, I will come again, and receive you unto Myself; that where I am, there ye may be also.' 'If ye love Me, keep My commandments. He that loveth Me not keepeth not My sayings.' 'I will pray the Father, and He shall give you another Comforter, that He may abide with you for ever; even the Spirit of Truth, whom the world cannot receive, because it seeth Him not, neither knoweth Him: but ye know Him; for He dwelleth with you, and shall be in you.'

'He shall be in you!' Working in the ethical world, invisible, except in results. Logically, cause must precede effect. This is an axiom which no man can gainsay; and man, having fallen by an act of disobedience to law, has to be restored to the image of God by being brought into obedience to law, the law of ethics. Why then does man turn a deaf ear to his Father's voice in Revelation, and refuse to recognise that Father's hand in creation? 'Because,' he virtually replies, 'I cannot see the necessity for anything higher than law, and I will not believe in anything of the existence of which there is no incontestable demonstration. When we have solved a few more difficult problems, and have improved our instruments, we shall know more, and we shall have acquired greater power to pursue our investigations, one result of which will be that we shall be enabled to make more use of the laws about which we already know so much.' Quite true; but, all the same, it is the story of Eden repeated through the ages; the story of disobedience to law, and of self-exaltation. Let a man once realize that he is made in the image of God, destined to live with God, and to work with Him, and then the pride of man dies a natural death; for, knowing what he is by the will of his Maker, while glorying, as he must do, in his unspeakable greatness, he will feel that he owes all to the God who made him, and breathed into him the breath of life: that Triune God who is his Creator, Redeemer, and Sanctifier.

The world is very evil, and 'strait is the gate, and narrow is the way that leadeth unto life, and few there be that find it.'

> 'Therefore, though few may praise, or help, or heed us,
>   Let us work on with head, or heart, or hand;
> For that we know the future ages need us,
>   And we must help our time to take its stand.
>
> 'Each single struggle hath its far vibration,
>   Working results that work results again;
> Failure and death are no annihilation,
>   Our tears exhaled will make some future rain.'*

---

* R. A. Vaughan.

CHAPTER III.

THE GREAT PROCESSION.*

In the 'Great Sacrament' God is discerned in the *material* world. In the 'Great Procession' He is manifested in the *spiritual* world. 'For,' as St. Paul says, 'the invisible things of Him from the creation of the world are clearly seen, being understood by the things that are made, even His eternal power and Godhead.'

The story of the creation of the material world has been told by men whose minds were Divinely illuminated. 'In the beginning God created the heaven and the earth. And the earth was without

---

* As so many passages from Holy Scripture are given in full at the commencement of this chapter, it seems desirable to state the reasons for this arrangement: (1) They are the strong foundation on which students of the 'Book of Nature' build the temple of truth, and learn the lesson that faith and science uphold each other, and are strong only in their union. (2) Many readers do not take the trouble to refer to texts when they are only indicated by figures. The Bible may not be at hand, or the time for reading may be limited, so that a study of the 'foundation' may be postponed until a more convenient season, which oftentimes never comes.

form and void; and darkness was upon the face of the deep: and the Spirit of God moved upon the face of the waters. And God said, Let there be light: and there was light. And God saw the light, that it was good: and God divided the light from the darkness. And God called the light day, and the darkness He called night.' This wonderful 'light' seems to have been the first glorious Epiphany, the Alpha that was to light, not the material world only, but also every man that cometh into the world; for, in later time, St. John wrote, 'In the beginning was the Word, and the Word was with God, and the Word was God. The same was in the beginning with God: all things were made by Him; and without Him was not anything made that was made. In Him was life, and the life was the light of men. And the light shineth in darkness, and the darkness comprehended it not.' When, according to the command of God, 'Moses stretched forth his hand toward heaven, there was a thick darkness in all the land of Egypt three days, so that the Egyptians saw not one another, neither rose any from his place for three days, but the children of Israel had light in their dwellings.' And those who can receive Holy Scripture as the 'Word of God'—knowing that 'no prophecy of the Scripture is of any private interpretation; for that prophecy came not in the old time by the will of man, but holy men of God spake as they were moved by the Holy Ghost'—see in this 'darkness' which came over Egypt, and this 'light' in the dwellings of the Hebrews, not only the working of Almighty power, but also emblems of the greater darkness by which the spirits of the Egyptians were surrounded when they bowed down before the gods which they themselves had made; and of the light, kindled by faith in the God of their fathers, which was ever burning in those Hebrew slaves. They seem to hear the cry of Isaiah, ' Arise, shine, for thy light is come, and the glory of the Lord is risen upon thee. For, behold, the darkness shall cover the earth, and gross darkness the people: but the Lord shall arise upon thee, and His glory shall be seen upon thee.' And St. Paul says, 'God, who commanded the light to shine out of darkness, is He who hath shined in our hearts, to give the light of the knowledge of the glory of God in the face of Jesus Christ. But we have this treasure in earthen vessels, that the excellency of the power may be of God, and not of us.'

Marvellously simple, as embodied in words inspired by Divine love, is this blending together of the seen and the unseen, of spirit and matter, of what is mortal and subject to change and decay, and of what is immortal and changeless.

Very wonderful and beautiful is the harmony which runs through Revelation. It appears wonderful to *us*, whose every-day life is spent in a world where sin has brought confusion. Yet man may attain to a suitable apprehension of it, if only he will have faith in God: for as 'in the beginning,' we are taught that life is light, and God the source of all, so at the close of God's written revelation to men, we read concerning the holy city, new Jerusalem, that it 'had no need of the sun, neither of the moon, to shine in it; for the glory of God did lighten it, and the Lamb is the light thereof.'

The sun of our solar system was not created with the 'Light.' Ages passed away during which eternal Wisdom was fashioning the earth, and making it ready to be the dwelling-place of man. Then God said, 'Let us make man in our image;' 'the Lord God formed man of the dust of the ground, and breathed into his nostrils the breath of life; and man became a living soul.' Not until He had created man, and given him dominion over the whole earth, did God rest from all His work which He had made: and then the great benediction was pronounced, which seems to typify the blessing which, from that day to the present, rests upon finished work well done. The life of each individual member of the human race, if lived as in the sight of God, will be blessed by the Maker of all; blessed with the rest of the seventh day; blessed with the 'rest that remaineth for the people of God.'

'Workmen of God ! oh, lose not heart,
    But learn what God is like ;
And in the darkest battlefield
    Thou shalt know where to strike.

'Thrice blest is he to whom is given
    The instinct that can tell
That God is on the field when He
    Is most invisible.

'Blest, too, is he who can divine
    Where real right doth lie,
And dares to take the side that seems
    Wrong to man's blindfold eye.

'Then learn to scorn the praise of men,
    And learn to lose with God ;
For Jesus won the world through shame,
    And beckons thee His road.

'For right is right, since God is God,
    And right the day must win ;
To doubt would be disloyalty,
    To falter would be sin.'*

God rested, satisfied with His last great work, Man: a being who is endowed with a lofty intellect, a mind that is capable of communing with his Creator, and a heart that can love Him—love even as God loved him ; for as all light is from God, so is all pure love in man a flame from the fire of love that is ever burning in the bosom of the Father. God rested. He saw everything that He had made, and behold, it was very good ; and God took Adam and put him into the Garden of Eden to dress it and to keep it, and gave to him all created good, with a power of free will to choose the good and refuse the

* Faber.

only thing that could harm him—namely, the experimental knowledge of evil. Evil existed before man was created, and the spirit of evil soon glided out of the darkness into the light, and the *rest* of God was broken, and the peace of Eden fled. Earth, henceforth, became a great battle-field; and through the centuries is heard from time to time, above the din of war, the piercing wail of the Divine Love, 'What could have been done more to my vineyard that I have not done in it?' 'Return unto Me.' 'Look unto Me, and be ye saved, all the ends of the earth.' 'Ho, everyone that thirsteth, come ye to the waters, and he that hath no money, come ye, buy and eat; yea, come, buy wine and milk, without money and without price.' 'O my people, what have I done unto thee? and wherein have I wearied thee? testify against me.' 'O Jerusalem, Jerusalem, how often would I have gathered thy children together, even as a hen gathereth her chickens under her wings, and ye would not.' Sin had come forth out of the darkness, and was casting its shadow upon what God had made so good. The glorious creation became a ruin, and man, the crown of creation, forfeited his inheritance, and sold his birthright for a mess of pottage. The dread sentence was pronounced, 'Dust thou art, and unto dust shalt thou return.' It was but for a brief space that the work of creation remained unsullied in the light of God, and only while it was so could

God rest. Sin must be overthrown and destroyed; and God 'put on righteousness as a breastplate, and a helmet of salvation upon His head; and He put on the garments of vengeance for clothing, and was clad with zeal as a cloak.' The work of redemption must be begun; and 'the Spirit of the Lord' lifted up a standard against the enemy that was coming in like a flood; and He said unto the serpent, the father of lies, 'Because thou hast done this, thou art cursed above all cattle, and above every beast of the field; upon thy belly shalt thou go, and dust shalt thou eat all the days of thy life. And I will put enmity between thee and the woman, and between thy seed and her seed; it shall bruise thy head, and thou shalt bruise his heel.'

The sentence pronounced by the holy and just Judge on man, and on the adversary of man, caused, as it were, an awful pause in the onward march of the 'Great Procession.' Adam and Eve, the offspring of united power and love, came next in order to the Three Persons of the Trinity. As the son and daughter of the King of the universe, children of God, and heirs of the Kingdom of Heaven, no created beings could excel them in dignity. In this age of the world, when assumption takes the place of truth, and the capricious lights of self-assertion are substituted for the lights of Revelation, of conscience, and of true philosophy; when man looks around him and surveys humanity in its fallen state, realizes its vileness, and hears so-called Christians consigning the great mass of mankind to the region of eternal torment—(where, in the words of Calvin, 'myriads of children with their toothless gums are crawling about the floor of hell'); when men are taught that the greatest sinner has nothing to do in order to be saved but to call upon the Lord Jesus, which is in direct contradiction to the teaching of the Divine Master, when He put the question, 'Why call ye Me, Lord, Lord, and do not the things which I say?'—in such an age, and face to face with the fact that man in the aggregate is utterly indifferent to, if not ignorant of, his high descent, his birthright privileges, his priceless inheritance, once forfeited, but now fully redeemed, purchased by the Sacrifice once offered for the sins of the whole world, it is only by asserting the dignity of man, showing him what he is in union with God, and what he has made himself by departing from God, that man can be raised from the depths to which he has fallen, and be put back into the path that leads to the height from which sin has drawn him.

The life of Jesus of Nazareth illustrates what perfect man is. The lives of the great majority of men give unmistakable evidence of what man has become since he allowed sin to intervene between him and his Maker. While he is content to rest under the dark shadow instead of striving to surmount it, and get once more into the sunlight of God's favour, he must be taught that, even in ruin, he is still a superhuman being, and that Christ died to redeem every individual soul. He must be made to realize that, in the sight of God, it matters not whether the soul tenants for a few brief years a body that is clothed in purple and fine linen, or one that is clothed in rags. As long as the miserable belief that is embodied in the words:

> 'Rattle his bones over the stones,
> It is only a pauper that nobody owns,'

is allowed to prevail in place of the Bible story of the poor man, who, when he died, was carried by the angels to Abraham's bosom; as long as the nobility and high mightiness of open sinners are engraved on marble, and praises are lavished upon them by the world of sycophants, the false estimate of man will prevail with the great mass of mankind, and check all effort to realize man's high destiny.

The origin of evil is known only to the ever-blessed Trinity. That it is the opposite of good we know; and, therefore, as God is good it is a departure from goodness; the will of a created intelligence opposed to the will of God. Any divergence from a perfect law would be, like the sin of Adam, a wilful act of disobedience if done by a reasonable creature, who is endowed with free will; and the result would be the same, whatever form the disobedience might take, because an element of disorder would thus invade God's system.

The 'war in heaven,' with the result that Satan and his angels were cast down to earth, and the fall of man, with the result that he was sent forth from Eden, prove that the law of cause and effect is constant, whether it is working among angels or among men. 'Spiritual wickedness in high places' had the same punishment awarded to it as spiritual wickedness in this lower world.

A false note in music destroys harmony; the breath of slander may blight the fairest character; a lie causes what is false to appear true. The first act of the great drama of human life enacted in Eden was related to the 'war in heaven,' in which 'Michael and his angels fought against the dragon, and the dragon fought, and his angels, and prevailed not; neither was their place found any more in heaven. And the great dragon was cast out, that old serpent called the devil, and Satan, which deceiveth the whole world: he was cast out into the earth, and his angels were cast out with him.' He fell, as the Lord Jesus tells us, 'like lightning from heaven,' and his first recorded act on earth was bringing the subtle influence of self-pleasing to bear upon the fairest creation of God. The tempter knew that he could reach the lord of creation through his wife, and so bring ruin and death upon them and their children. His superhuman subtilty enabled him to accomplish his design; but the mystery which the angels have desired to look into was hidden from him. He did not know, in the hour of his triumph, that God Himself would come down from heaven to snatch the prey from his hand, and redeem the human race: that although in His justice He must punish the sin, He would, in His love and mercy, and according to His predetermined purpose, save the sinner; and eventually cast sin and death into the lake of fire, the eternal fire of God's wrath against sin.

Too often in these days of modern thought the intellect of man attempts in various ways to account for sin, and even to explain it away or cast a veil over it, and make it appear less hateful than it is; but the universality, and the dread working of sin, changing as it does the sons and daughters of God into slaves of self, cause all those who are striving to overcome sin in themselves, and who are helping others to fight against it, to regard it as the most terrible reality of life. Everyone may say with St. Paul, ' I find then a law that, when I would do good, evil is present with me. For I delight in the law of God after the inward man: but I see another law in my members, warring against the law of my mind, and bringing me into captivity to the law of sin which is in my members. O, wretched man that I am! who shall deliver me from this body of death?' But he adds, 'I thank

God through Jesus Christ our Lord. There is therefore now no condemnation to them which are in Christ Jesus, who walk not after the flesh but after the Spirit. For the law of the Spirit of life in Christ Jesus hath made me free from the law of sin and death.' This Christ was the seed of the woman that was to bruise the serpent's head by the law of sacrifice—the absolute and entire surrender of self. The words, 'I came not to do Mine own will, but the will of Him who sent Me,' epitomise the life of Him who died on Calvary; and that perfect Sacrifice secured the redemption of a lost world, overcame sin and death, and opened heaven to man. In like manner the yielding up of our will to God, so that whether in sickness or in health, in storm or in sunshine, we can say, 'Not my will, but Thine be done,' gives *us*, in, through, and by Christ, all power in heaven and on earth; a share of Christ's glory; a seat on His judgment throne; and it ensures the welcome 'Come, ye blessed of My Father, inherit the kingdom prepared for you.' Well may St. Paul say, 'For our light affliction, which is but for a moment, worketh for us a far more exceeding and eternal weight of glory; while we look not at the things which are seen, but at the things which are not seen; for the things which are seen are temporal; but the things which are not seen are eternal.'

But before man can enter Canaan he has to pass

through the wilderness, as our ancestors did when they left Eden. Even in its uncultured state it was a beautiful wilderness. Thorns and thistles, indeed, sprang up in their path, because the ground was cursed for Adam's sin; but the unchangeable Jehovah having from the beginning loved the creature He had made in His own image, loved on with patient pitying love; and His smile was seen in the sunlight, which caused the flowers to grow wherever a tear of penitence fell.

Next in the long procession walked Cain and Abel, inheritors of that gift of free will, by the misuse of which Adam and Eve had fallen. Each was capable of loving and obeying God, or of turning away from Him and disobeying Him. Each could walk through the wilderness in the narrow path of obedience under the guidance of the Holy Spirit, or could turn into the broad plane that stretched out on either side, and there be a law unto himself and the slave of his own self-will. In the persons of Cain and Abel we have typical representatives of the bad and good in all ages. Each child of earth when he joins the great procession has to choose under whose banner he will march in the war; for fight he must, either for God or against Him. According to the choice he makes will be his future weal or woe. 'A good man out of the good treasure of his heart bringeth forth good things; and an evil man out of the evil treasure bringeth forth evil things.' And so it was that when the brothers offered their sacrifices to the Lord the sacrifice of Abel was accepted, and the sacrifice of Cain was rejected; for we are told that, 'the Lord had respect unto Abel and to his offering, but unto Cain and to his offering He had not respect.' The reason for the rejection of Cain's offering is explained: 'If thou doest well, shalt thou not be accepted? and if thou doest not well, sin lieth at the door.' Face to face with sin stood Cain, free to refuse the evil and choose the good. God would not keep him from opening the door of his heart and taking sin in, because that would involve an interference with the free will on which the moral quality of human actions depends. In the case of Abel sin was not 'lying at the door,' and thus he was able to present a sacrifice that was acceptable unto God; and he was pronounced 'righteous.'

So, from the beginning, we see the power of the 'invisible' controlling and directing the 'visible.' Man sees only the outward acts; God looks into the heart. Wise men, in this era of free-thought and moral declension, tell us that our offerings can be of no value in the eyes of a purely spiritual God; that our gold, and silver, and precious stones, the rich adornment of churches erected for God's glory and the good of men, are but so many evidences of æsthetic taste, and are a wasteful expenditure of time and money. We would have them remember the story of Cain and Abel; the building of Solomon's Temple in all its magnificent details, under the directions of the Architect of the universe; and that touching episode in the life of one whose name is written in the 'Lamb's Book of Life,' but who is only known on earth as a poor widow who cast into the treasury of God's house in Jerusalem all that she possessed. God is a Spirit, and looks into the heart; and this fact is, as it were, the key that unlocks the door of the council-chamber of Deity, and enables us to see and understand a little of God's ways, which are not as man's ways. His thoughts are higher than man's thoughts, and so He sees what is to Him the priceless offering of a pure, loving intention where man sees only a sculptured entablature. He sees an act of adoration to the Lamb where man sees but a golden chalice. He sees a longing desire to do something for His glory and honour, where man sees only a costly edifice. He sees the sacrifice of self, where man sees but a widow's mite. Hence it was that Abel's offering found favour with God, and Cain's was rejected. The outward and visible sign of sacrifice was in Cain's offering, but the inward and spiritual grace was not there; and *both* are required by God, as Christ taught, when He said to the Pharisees: 'Woe unto you Scribes and Pharisees, hypocrites! for ye pay tithe of mint, and anise, and cummin, and have omitted the weightier matters of the law, judgment, mercy, and faith; these ought ye to have done, and not to leave the other undone.' With the firstling of his flock, Abel offered also his heart. Cain made the material offering, but not the spiritual; thus rendering the material offering of no avail. As it was then, so it is now; each member of the human family must follow after either Cain or Abel. He must choose for himself whether, at the 'end of the days,' he will stand on the right hand or on the left of the Judge; and whether, while marching on through the wilderness, he will keep in spiritual darkness, or walk in the light of obedience, love, and sacrifice.

As men multiplied on the earth, the great procession lengthened, and one generation after another passed out of sight; but the ranks of the army have ever remained unbroken, and like the windings of a mighty river, it moves on ceaselessly through successive ages. 'Not lost, but gone before,' is what we say of the vanguard who, no doubt, are conscious of the far-stretching column that is marching in the way their steps have trod; and those who are in the rear know that they too must one day let go the material mantle, and join the advanced guard. 'How long, O Lord! holy, and true, dost Thou not judge, and avenge our blood on them that dwell on the earth?' was the cry of the souls that St. John saw under the altar, who had been slain for the word of God, and for the testimony which they held. 'And white robes were given unto every one of them; and it was said unto them, that they should rest yet for a little season, until their fellow-servants also, and their brethren, that should be killed as they were, should be fulfilled.' And then St. John, the beloved disciple—to whom, doubtless, such great revelations of the unseen universe were vouchsafed because of the great love he bore to his Divine Master, and of his faithfulness to the Crucified One when all the other apostles forsook Him and fled—he, the faithful and true witness, tells of 'a great multitude which no man could number, of all nations, and kindreds, and tongues,' standing 'before the throne, and before the Lamb, clothed with white robes, and palms in their hands;' and he heard them crying with a loud voice, saying, 'Salvation to our God which sitteth upon the throne, and unto the Lamb.' And one of the elders which stood with the angels round about the throne, told St. John that those who were arrayed in white robes, were 'they which came out of great tribulation, and had washed their robes, and made them white in the blood of the Lamb.' 'Therefore are they before the throne of God, and serve Him day and night in His temple, and He that sitteth on the throne shall dwell among them. They shall hunger no more, neither thirst any more; neither shall the sun light on them, nor any heat. For the Lamb which is in the midst of the throne shall feed them, and shall lead them unto living fountains of waters; and God shall wipe away all tears from their eyes.'

St. John also writes : ' I saw in the right hand of Him that sat on the throne a book, written within and on the backside, sealed with seven seals. And I saw a strong angel proclaiming with a loud voice, Who is worthy to open the book, and to loose the seals thereof? And no man in heaven, nor in earth, neither under the earth, was able to open the book, neither to look thereon. And I wept much, because no man was found worthy to open and to read the book, neither to look thereon. And one of the elders'— one, it may be, of 'the noble army of martyrs,' or of 'the goodly fellowship of the prophets,' or of the long line of confessors—' saith unto me, Weep not : behold, the Lion of the tribe of Judah, the Root of David, hath prevailed to open the book, and to loose the seven seals thereof. And I beheld, and lo, in the midst of the throne, and of the four beasts, and in the midst of the elders, stood a Lamb as it had been slain, having seven horns and seven eyes, which are the seven Spirits of God sent forth into all the earth. And He came and took the book out of the right hand of Him that sat upon the throne. And when He had taken the book, the four beasts and the four and twenty elders fell down before the Lamb, having everyone of them harps, and golden vials full of odours, which are the prayers of saints. And they sung a new song, saying, Thou art worthy to take the book, and to open the seals thereof: for Thou wast slain, and hast redeemed us to God by Thy blood, out of every kindred, and tongue, and people, and nation; and hast made us unto our God kings and priests, and we shall reign on the earth. And I beheld, and I heard the voice of many angels round about the throne, and the beasts, and the elders: and the number of them was ten thousand times ten thousand, and thousands of thousands; saying with a loud voice, Worthy is the Lamb that was slain to receive power, and riches, and wisdom, and strength, and honour, and glory, and blessing. And every creature which is in heaven, and on the earth, and such as are in the sea, and all that are in them heard I saying, Blessing, and honour, and glory, and power, be unto Him that sitteth upon the throne, and unto the Lamb for ever and ever. And the four beasts said, Amen. And the four and twenty elders fell down and worshipped Him that liveth for ever and ever.'

Among that great multitude, we may feel sure that Enoch, who 'walked with God,' was numbered; also Noah, who 'found grace in the eyes of the Lord,' when all flesh had corrupted his way upon the earth, and the earth was filled with violence; for he was one of the three upright men distinguished by God Himself, who, when the house of Israel had set up idols in their hearts, and polluted the land by their iniquities, said to Ezekiel, 'Son of man, when the land sinneth against Me by trespassing grievously, then will I stretch out My hand upon it, and will cut off man and beast from it; though Noah, Daniel, and Job were in it, they should deliver but their own souls by their righteousness.'

The apostle defines faith to be 'the substance (or ground) of things hoped for, the evidence of things not seen. For by it the elders obtained a good report. Through faith we understand that the worlds were framed by the word of God, so that things which are seen were not made of things which do appear.' 'Without faith'—the faith that overcometh the world and its temptations, the faith of the Son of God—'it is impossible to please God.' 'By faith Abel offered unto God a more excellent sacrifice than Cain, by which he obtained witness that he was righteous, God testifying of his gifts: and by it he being dead yet speaketh. By faith Enoch was translated that he should not see death; and was not found, because God had translated him: for before his translation he had this testimony, that he pleased God.' 'By faith Noah, being warned of God of things not seen as yet, moved with fear, prepared an ark to the saving of his house; by the which he condemned the world, and became heir of the righteousness which is by faith. By faith Abraham, when he was called to go out into a place which he should after receive for an inheritance, obeyed; and he went out, not knowing whither he went. By faith he sojourned in the land of promise, as in a strange country, dwelling in tabernacles with Isaac and Jacob, the heirs with him of the same promise: For he looked for a city which hath foundations, whose builder and maker is God. Through faith also Sara herself received strength to conceive seed, and was delivered of a child when she was past age, because she judged Him faithful who had promised. Therefore sprang there even of one, and him as good as dead, so many as the stars of the sky in multitude, and as the sand which is by the sea shore innumerable. These all died according to faith, not having received the promises, but having seen them afar off, and were persuaded of them, and embraced them, and confessed that they were strangers and pilgrims on the earth. For they that say such things declare plainly that they seek a country. And truly, if they had been mindful of that country from whence they came out, they might have had opportunity to have returned. But now they desire a better country, that is, an heavenly: wherefore God is not ashamed to be called their God: for He hath prepared for them a city. By faith Abraham, when he was tried, offered up Isaac: and he that had received the promises offered up his only begotten son, of whom it was said, That in

Isaac shall thy seed be called: accounting that God was able to raise him up, even from the dead; from whence also he received him in a figure. By faith Isaac blessed Jacob and Esau concerning things to come. By faith Jacob when he was a dying, blessed both the sons of Joseph; and worshipped, leaning upon the top of his staff. By faith Joseph, when he died, made mention of the departing of the children of Israel; and gave commandment concerning his bones. By faith Moses, when he was born, was hid three months of his parents, because they saw he was a proper child; and they were not afraid of the king's commandment. By faith Moses, when he was come to years, refused to be called the son of Pharaoh's daughter; choosing rather to suffer affliction with the people of God, than to enjoy the pleasures of sin for a season; esteeming the reproach of Christ greater riches than the treasures in Egypt: for he had respect unto the recompense of the reward. By faith he forsook Egypt, not fearing the wrath of the king: for he endured as seeing Him who is invisible. Through faith he kept the passover, and the sprinkling of blood, lest he that destroyed the firstborn should touch them. By faith they passed through the Red sea as by dry land: which the Egyptians assaying to do were drowned. By faith the walls of Jericho fell down, after they were compassed about seven days. By faith the harlot

Rahab perished not with them that believed not, when she had received the spies with peace.'

'And what,' adds the writer of this Epistle, 'shall I more say? for the time would fail me to tell of Gideon, and of Barak, and of Samson, and of Jephthah; of David also, and Samuel, and of the prophets; who through faith subdued kingdoms, wrought righteousness, obtained promises, stopped the mouths of lions, quenched the violence of fire, escaped the edge of the sword, out of weakness were made strong, waxed valiant in fight, turned to flight the armies of the aliens. Women received their dead raised to life again, and others were tortured, not accepting deliverance, that they may obtain a better resurrection; and others had trial of cruel mockings and scourgings, yea, moreover of bonds, and imprisonment: they were stoned, they were sawn asunder, were tempted, were slain with the sword: they wandered about in sheep-skins and goat-skins; being destitute, afflicted, tormented; (of whom the world was not worthy:) they wandered in deserts, and in mountains, and in dens and caves of the earth. And these all, having obtained a good report through faith, received not the promise, God having provided some better thing for us, that they without us should not be made perfect.' 'Wherefore seeing we also are compassed about with so great a cloud of witnesses, let us lay aside every weight and the sin that doth so easily beset us, and let us run with patience the race that is set before us: looking unto Jesus, the author and finisher of our faith; who for the joy that was set before Him endured the cross, despising the shame, and is set down at the right hand of the throne of God.'

St. John wrote, for the edification of the Church, which is the body of Christ, of the state of the blessed dead, who, with the Crucified, are alive for evermore in a house not made with hands, eternal in the heavens: and this author wrote of those servants of God, who were remarkable types of the varying characters of all who, in succeeding generations, should tread in their footsteps; and by their example of faith and good works, lead others to live such lives on earth as would prepare them for the life of glory and happiness which was revealed through St. John, in order that we may know a little of what God has prepared for those that love Him. 'Eye hath not seen, nor ear heard; neither hath it entered into the heart of man' to conceive all the exceeding glory.

It is a comfort and a joy to know that the way in which the soldiers of the Cross have to walk now is no new or untrodden path. Though strait and narrow, it is wide enough for all who choose to walk in it. It is a royal road, and along it have all the saints of God walked from the days of 'righteous Abel' unto the present time. On the line of march, have been, and shall be seen, even unto the end, prophets, priests, and kings; apostles, confessors, and virgins; a noble army of martyrs, living as strangers and pilgrims. They turn from the allurements of the world, as Moses did in old time, and they endure the trials of life, as becomes soldiers of the Cross, and as seeing Him who to mortal sight is invisible ; but who to the eye of faith is always a present help in times of adversity, as near to each one who calls upon Him in the hour of sorrow as He was to the sisters of Lazarus, when He said unto them, 'Thy brother shall rise again.'

There are many battalions in the army, and as the procession passes on, we see by the movements of the soldiers, and by the device upon the banners which they carry, the object which they are striving to attain. At one period of the world's history, men attempted to build a city, and a tower whose top should reach to heaven. 'Let us,' they said, 'make us a name, lest we be scattered abroad upon the face of the whole earth'; and the followers of those who began to build their tower of fame on the plain of Shinar, still plant, and build, and call the land after their own name, forgetting that here they have 'no continuing city,' and that the banner of worldly pride which they vauntingly display is unfurled in an enemy's country, and that at any moment the work they have begun may totter and fall.

Other divisions of the army are content to gather the flowers, and the weeds with them, that grow in their path; and so subtle are the attacks of the great enemy of man that they often escape the observation of these easy souls. Endowed with all the knowledge and power of an Archangel, Satan comes forth from the darkness armed with various weapons. To all who range themselves under the banner of the Cross, he transforms himself into an angel of light, using different devices to turn them aside from the strait way in which their Captain walked.

There are others in the Great Procession who are content with present ease and luxury; who wander listlessly on into the future, without any definite purpose; taking for their motto, 'Let us eat and drink, for to-morrow we die.' No need for the fallen archangel to transform himself into an angel of light in order to deceive *them*. The sunlight of to-day is enough for them, and in that light they stroll about, gathering while the morning lasts all that pleases the senses; but even at noon the light begins to grow dim for them, and, with a sigh of regret that the brightness of the early hours has faded, that all has lost its freshness, or has perished in the using, they begin to store up more lasting treasures, gold and silver, and precious stones, or 'knowledge that puffeth up,' without elevating. All earth's treasures, gathered and used *only* for time and self, without any recognition of the higher part of man's being, with all its duties and responsibilities, are but barriers which shut out the light from heaven; and all who are satisfied to rest behind those barriers are far away from the Source of light. It is only when one of the sleepers is aroused, discovers that he is groping in darkness, and raises his eyes to catch a glimpse of a brighter world, that the evil one draws near to tempt him to close his eyes again, and take his rest. Such as these were the people whom Moses led out of Egypt. By the power and might of the Lord the children of Israel had been delivered from a bondage that was too heavy for them to bear. Their taskmasters had been slain by the pestilence, or drowned in the Red Sea, and danger was past. They had but to walk through the wilderness of Shur, hearkening diligently to the voice of God, who spoke by Moses, in order to reach the land of rest and promise. Stiffnecked and perverse, however, they soon proved to be, and began to murmur—'Would to God we had died by the hand of the Lord in the land of Egypt, when we sat by the flesh-pots, and when we did eat bread to the full.' Faithless, after all the wonders which had been wrought for their deliverance, they cried out to Moses and Aaron, and said, 'Ye have brought us forth into this wilderness, to kill this whole assembly with hunger.' And Moses said, 'Your murmurings are not against us, but against the Lord.' Being merciful and gracious, long-suffering, and full of compassion and pity, the Lord answered their murmuring with a blessing, 'Behold, I will rain bread from heaven for you, and ye shall know that I am the Lord your God.' 'And in the morning the dew lay round about the host; and when the dew that lay was gone up, behold, upon the face of the wilderness there lay a small round thing, as small as the hoar-frost on the ground. And when the children of Israel saw it, they said one to another, It is a portion; for they knew not what it was. And Moses said unto them, This is the bread which the Lord hath given you to eat.'

Thus has the great Father ever dealt with man from the beginning, yet man still provokes Him every day. Man is ever changing, but, in majestic silence, the unchangeable God develops His will, and unfolds His plan, for the salvation of man; and the records of the past, and a careful observation of the present, alike bear witness to the fact that is embodied in the words, 'History repeats itself.' There is the inevitable fate of nations typefied in the individual life of each man; the rise and fall of one, the youth and old age of the other. There is no standing still, even for a moment, although there is often a seeming pause in the working of the fixed, but ever active laws which govern the universe. There is what is called the prime of man's life, when the physical part of his being has ceased to grow, and when the unseen ripening of nature goes on until full maturity is reached; and then, unseen, the slow, sure decadence begins, the end of which is death. So also it is with nations. They have small beginnings: each rises as an oak does from the acorn; each increases in might and power, and knowledge, and dominion, until the highest point is attained, and then, as surely as a mountaineer when he has reached the greatest altitude has to descend to the common level, the downward course begins. This law of progression and retrogression is universal; but among 'all the changes and chances of this mortal life' God's servants have ever found strength and rest, and peace, in the unchangeableness of Him who fed His rebellious children in the wilderness with the manna that was typical of that bread from heaven, with which we are fed in the Blessed Sacrament of the altar. The bread from heaven that was given to the Israelites nourished the mortal body. The bread which God gave in later days gives life to the soul. Just as the bond between us and the first Adam is our fleshly descent, so the bond between us and the second Adam is in the two great sacraments of Baptism and the Lord's Supper. By Baptism we are grafted into the Vine—the Living Vine—and thus, mystically, each becomes a living branch, a child of God, a member of Christ, and an heir of the kingdom of heaven. By the Eucharist, our union with Him who said, 'I am the Bread of Life,' is sustained and strengthened, for when Jesus said to His disciples, 'I am that Bread of Life,' He added, 'Your fathers did eat manna in the wilderness, and are dead. This is the Bread which cometh down from heaven, that a man may eat thereof, and not die.'

None will know, until the day dawns when all secrets shall be revealed, what an increase of spiritual vitality is given to each faithful worshipper at the Eucharist: none can measure the extent of the loss which all who will not receive the Bread of Life must sustain. The unseen is not yet unveiled; but when man considers the emblem, and what were the results of not gathering the manna in the wilderness—where no other food to sustain animal life was to be had—to the Hebrews, he cannot escape from the conclusion, that refusing to eat the 'Living Bread,' that comes down from heaven at every celebration of the Blessed Sacrament, must have an awful effect upon his spiritual and immortal life. In the strength which the Bread of Life gives, man may make giant-strides in the spiritual life; but without spiritual food how can the spirit of man grow? One of the saddest sights the sun shines upon is that of a human being choosing evil and refusing good; living for the things of time, and giving no thought to the things of eternity.

The history of the children of Israel was written for man's learning; and from first to last it is, in a general way, typical of national and individual life. The descendants of Jacob became slaves and bondmen in the land of Egypt, and burdens were laid upon them which were greater than they could bear. In the midst of all the wealth and glory of Egypt, the sons and daughters of Israel were trodden in the dust; and all the learning and wisdom of the Egyptians only seemed to harden their hearts against these Hebrew slaves. Nevertheless Israelites continued to multiply, according to the word of the Lord, who had appeared unto their forefather Abram, when he was ninety and nine years old, and when Isaac, the son of promise, was not, and said unto him, 'I am the Almighty God; walk before Me, and be thou perfect. And I will make My covenant between Me and thee, and will multiply thee exceedingly. As for Me, behold, My covenant is with thee, and thou shalt be a father of a multitude of nations. Neither shall thy name any more be called Abram, but thy name shall be Abraham; for a father of many nations have I made thee. And I will make thee exceeding fruitful, and I will make nations of thee, and kings shall come out of thee. And I will establish My covenant between Me and thee and thy seed after thee in their generations for an everlasting covenant, to be a God unto thee and to thy seed after thee. And I will give unto thee, and to thy seed after thee, the land of thy sojournings, all the land of Canaan, for an everlasting possession, and I will be their God.' And the word of the Lord was fulfilled. As time rolled on the Israelites increased abundantly, and 'waxed exceeding mighty,' and the land of Egypt was filled with them. And the king of Egypt saw that the children of the captivity were more in numbers and mightier than the Egyptians, and he ordered the taskmasters to afflict them: but the more they afflicted them the more they multiplied and grew, until Pharaoh in fear and wrath commanded that all the men-children should be destroyed as soon as they were born. Then it was that God Himself came to their rescue. He heard their groaning, and remembered His covenant with Abraham, with Isaac, and with Jacob; and He raised up Moses to deliver them from bondage, and lead them forth out of Egypt.

Marvellous are the revelations of superhuman power, bringing about the fulfilment of prophecy, and the accomplishment of God's designs, in the history of the Hebrew nation. God's will is supreme. His will was that Israel's children should dwell in Canaan, and become a great nation, innumerable as the stars, or the sand upon the sea-shore. He did not show Himself unto Pharaoh; He worked through Moses: and so it came to pass that one man, and he one of the captive race, confronted the might of Egypt, and triumphed gloriously. Well might Moses ask, 'Who am I, that I should go unto Pharaoh, and that I should bring forth the children of Israel out of Egypt?' God had called him by name, and appeared unto him on Mount Horeb, and said, 'I am the God of thy father, the God of Abraham, the God of Isaac, and the God of Jacob. I have surely seen the affliction of my people which are in Egypt, and have heard their cry by reason of their task-masters, for I know their sorrows; and I am come down to deliver them out of the hands of the Egyptians, and to bring them out of that land unto a good land and a large, unto a land flowing with milk and honey. Come now, therefore, and I will send thee unto Pharaoh, that thou mayest bring forth My people, the children of Israel, out of Egypt.' Who would not fall down and hide his face, and be afraid, and cry, as Moses did, 'Who am I that I should go unto Pharaoh, and that I should bring forth the children of Israel out of Egypt?' But God answered him, 'Certainly I will be with thee.' In the unseen presence of the Lord of Hosts with Moses was all-sufficient strength. When His arm is stretched out to save or to destroy, none can resist. 'Go,' said the Almighty to His chosen servant,

'Go, and gather the elders of Israel together, and say unto them, The Lord God of your fathers, the God of Abraham, of Isaac, and of Jacob, appeared unto me, saying, I have surely visited you, and seen that which is done to you in Egypt; and I have said I will bring you up out of the affliction of Egypt unto a land flowing with milk and honey: and they shall hearken to thy voice, and thou shalt come, thou and the elders of Israel unto the king of Egypt, and ye shall say unto him, The Lord God of the Hebrews hath met with us : and now let us go, we beseech thee, three days' journey into the wilderness, that we may sacrifice to the Lord our God. And I am sure that the king of Egypt will not let you go, but by a strong hand. And I will stretch out My hand, and smite Egypt with all My wonders which I will do in the midst thereof: and after that he will let you go.' Still Moses feared, and said, 'But, behold, they will not believe me, nor hearken unto my voice : for they will say, The Lord hath not appeared unto thee.' And God, full of love and compassion, vouchsafed signs to strengthen His servant's faith. But again Moses faltered, and said, 'O my Lord, I am not eloquent, neither heretofore, nor since thou hast spoken unto Thy servant : but I am slow of speech, and of a slow tongue.' And the Lord said unto him, 'Who hath made man's mouth? or who maketh the dumb, or deaf, or the seeing, or the blind? Have not I the Lord? Now, therefore, go, and I will be with thy mouth, and teach thee what thou shalt say.' Even this was not enough, and once more Moses trembled and feared, not realizing that he was but the favoured instrument in God's hand for accomplishing the great work set before him. And he said 'O my Lord, send, I pray thee, by the hand of him whom Thou shouldest send. And the anger of the Lord was kindled against Moses; and he said, Is not Aaron the Levite thy brother? I know that he can speak well. And thou shalt speak unto him, and put words in his mouth: and I will be with thy mouth and with his mouth, and will teach you what ye shall do. And he shall be thy spokesman unto the people: and he shall be, even he shall be to thee instead of a mouth, and thou shalt be to him instead of God.'

The king of Egypt withstood Moses; for he knew not that One greater than all the gods of Egypt was present with him. Plague after plague was brought upon the land, yet the king hardened his heart, and not until all the first-born of the Egyptians, from the first-born of Pharaoh that sat upon the throne, unto the first-born of the captive that was in the dungeon, lay dead, did the proud monarch of Egypt call for Moses and Aaron, and bid them 'Rise up, and go forth from among the Egyptians.' If no unseen Power had been directing and overruling all, why should a Pharaoh endure the presence of Moses, and parley with him about his slaves and bondmen? Slaves are always unarmed, and, therefore, numerous as were the Hebrews, they were, humanly speaking, powerless in the land of their captivity, surrounded as they were by their captors, the mightiest warriors in the world, and unmatched in discipline and power.

It was a great deliverance that was wrought, apparently by Moses; as in after years another great victory was gained by a youth with a sling and a stone; and as in modern days England owes her greatness and her vast dominions to the genius of her Saxon King, Alfred. And the world says that 'chance,' or 'a favourable combination of circumstances,' or 'causes which could be easily explained, if we had the means of ascertaining all the facts, brought about these results which appear to be so wonderful, but are in themselves only the natural outcome of the exercise of man's power and free will.' These are some of man's sophisms; the vague, unscientific propositions which are put forth by men who pride themselves upon believing no more than they can see and understand. Ask them how they know that they are living men, and they would probably say that reason assured them of the fact. But we cannot reason about a thing that is not; we must have reason before we can use it; and the perception of that fact, a knowledge of the possession of reason, is a passive act of faith.

Faith is the gift of God, we are distinctly told; and because it is His gift, and because of its inestimable value, as the foundation on which all good works must be built up in order to be acceptable to God—for we must believe in Him before we can love and serve Him—the author of evil uses all these delusions to blind man to the truth. Well he knows from his own experience how subtle is the influence of the pride of intellect; and how easy and natural it is to man in his fallen state to elevate reason into the place of Him who bestowed it upon man: and, therefore, to minds of the highest order, Satan hides from view the grosser forms of evil, and works at undermining faith in the Author and Giver of all good. But Hope, one of the brightest stars in the firmament of Earth, shines clear and steady, and is more lustrous when the night is darkest.

The evil which we know exists, and which has some mysterious connection with the exercise of free will, is allowed by God to develop all its hideous deformity and to injure mankind, not with a view to its final destruction, but for its ultimate good. God's *ways* are past finding out; but His *plan* of salvation has been declared. Sin, and death which is the result of sin, are to be destroyed. The sinner is to be saved by the power of the great Sacrifice, God Himself taking our flesh as a veil, and in that flesh dying for man. All this is matter of history to us. The salvation of man has been accomplished. 'It is finished,' and in the light of fulfilled prophecy, and of historical evidence, the sinfulness of that want of faith which excited God's anger against Moses is small, indeed, compared with the sin of this age. When we read of the task that was set before Moses, and think of its vastness, and of the weakness of the instrument that was to be used for its accomplishment: when we realize that the work was to be done in an enemy's country, and that all the power of the king and of a great nation were arrayed against the one man who was called by the unseen King of kings to stand before Pharaoh, and demand the release of the builders of the treasure-cities; then—as we look around and see the 'little faith' which only seems to flicker in this our day of grace—we cease to wonder at Moses losing heart and entreating God to send another to do the work. In a later period of man's history another servant of God besought the Lord for relief from pain, and he was told, 'My grace is sufficient for thee; for My strength is made perfect in weakness.' When Moses did 'put his hand to the plough' he became one of the most signal examples of the way in which the natural man can be sustained by the Divine Power. The great exodus from Egypt, and all the wonders which preceded it, were wrought by the Divine Power working through Moses. The passage of the Red Sea completed the deliverance of the Hebrews, and then followed the forty years of wandering in the wilderness. It is a sad and humiliating story, one of murmuring idolatry and rebellion on the part of man : one of patient forbearance, long-suffering and forgiveness, with just, yet loving, retribution and punishment of sin on the part of God.

We are all too prone to regard the lives of the men and women of Holy Scripture as quite different to our own lives; the actors in the scenes that are sketched do not seem to be really like the men and women of all the ages. But surely the men and women of old time would be such as we are if they were living now; and we should have been like them, and have done very much as they did, if we had lived in their time. God made man upright. When by reason of sin man lost his uprightness he became subject to changes; the conditions of his life were altered. The more he allowed sin to reign over him the more confusion and disorder prevailed; the farther he departed from the counsels of God the less able he became to govern himself wisely and with due self-control; the less able he was either to obey those who had the earthly rule over him, or to be content with that state of life in which God had placed him. The oldest records of the past, and the state of the world at the present moment, demonstrate this fact; and if we follow the stream of history from its source until we reach the stormy sea on which man is now sailing—talking of peace while preparing for war; preaching righteousness and working iniquity; boasting of civilization and refinement, while the few have the wealth of Crœsus and the many are starving and helpless, some dying like dogs within a stone's-throw of gorgeous palaces—we shall find that it has always been the same, and that it will be so to the end of time; for, as we have seen, the laws which govern the universe are as unchangeable as the God who made them. If we bear in mind that man *is* man, and can be neither more nor less than man, whether he be cultured as a Plato or degraded as a savage; that he was made a free-agent, and that evil has dogged his steps from the beginning, we shall more clearly understand the records of sacred and profane history, and the life of the Hebrews in the wilderness.

During the centuries that elapsed from the time when Joseph ruled in Egypt, the descendants of Israel must (this is suggested by the episode of the golden calves) have partly lost faith in the God of Israel, and adopted something of the idolatrous worship of Egypt. They received the law of God from Moses as we receive it from the 'Holy Catholic Church;' and, as many members of Christ's body do now, regarding the Church as *merely* a human institution, whose laws and teaching may be accepted or rejected at pleasure, they failed to see beyond the veil, and to acknowledge God in Moses; they did as men do now, condemned His action and rebelled against His authority. The result of all their sin and disobedience was that out of the great multitude of free men who came from Egypt, only two survived to enter the Promised Land. All the others died in the wilderness. But what an inglorious ending to the march that was commenced in the land of the Pharaohs was the death of one after another of that long procession in the wilderness! What a sad ending of life in this world is indicated by the words, 'Many are called, but few are chosen.' Only eight were saved when the flood came, and the waters covered the earth. Only one family escaped from the doomed cities of the plain, the rest perished. History tells of great nations, and of their kings and mighty men of valour, who have long since passed away; and ruined monuments that were raised thousands of years ago testify still to the lofty conceptions of the designers, and the cultured skill of the workmen, but remain only to attest the truth of the saying, 'There is nothing new under the sun.' The greatest empires and kingdoms of the world have risen and fallen; and the countless generations of men who thought and worked and toiled as men do now, who gathered and stored vast treasures of wisdom and knowledge, or who fought for their country and their king as bravely as the sons of Britain fight for the honour of England to-day, are all gone, vanished from mortal sight. Through successive ages the verdict of history is the same—but few are ever found walking in the narrow way; the many are in the broad road. Not ten righteous men were to be found in Sodom. Not many righteous kings ruled over God's chosen people. The true prophets of God who were sent to warn men of coming punishment if they continued to rebel against the laws of God were persecuted, imprisoned, and afflicted: others prophesied falsely, and 'the people loved to have it so.' Each great national history has its good king, its Daniel, and its apostle of truth; but of the vast majority it seems to be written: 'they are weighed in the balance and found wanting.'

There is no material difference, except that which diversity of taste and changing circumstances make, between the people of ancient Tyre, or Capernaum, and the wealthy inhabitants of the cities of modern Europe. There is the same costly magnificence in their attire, and in the adornment of their palaces; the same pride of life; the same careless ease and love of the world; and the same immorality. Where one searches for and finds the 'Pearl of great price,' and stretches forth hand and heart to grasp it, thousands are content to possess a few poor pearls of present self-pleasing. Where one strives for the 'laurel crown,' thousands are content to wear wreaths of flowers that fade well-nigh as soon as gathered. Where one soldier fights for God and the right, thousands lay aside their armour and live at ease. Is then, the vast army lost? Is the hand of the Lord shortened that it cannot save? Is the standard of victory snatched from the hand of the Captain of our salvation in the final loss of the great majority? If so, heaven will be thinly peopled, and some of the many mansions prepared for the children of men in the kingdom of their Father will be empty: and the God-man will have few of those whom He has made brothers and sisters, by taking human flesh and dwelling among them, with Him in His home above. Has God cast off the great multitude of those whom He delivered from Egyptian bondage for ever? Are the wanderers never to reach home, never to find a place of rest? Are all the Jews who have lived with the veil upon their hearts during the past nineteen centuries, thus demonstrating the truth of prophecy, and proclaiming by their continued existence as a separate nation, that God rules on earth, and shapes the destiny of men, to be lost? Are only those who shall be alive when Christ once more stands upon Mount Zion to be converted and saved? The prayer of the dying Saviour gives the answer. 'Father, forgive them, for they know not what they do.' 'As in Adam all die, even so in Christ shall all be made alive.'

'At the name of Jesus every knee shall bow, of things in heaven, and things in earth, and things under the earth; and every tongue shall confess that Jesus Christ is Lord to the glory of God the Father.' 'All that go down to the dust shall bow before Him.' 'All the ends of the world shall remember and turn unto the Lord; and all the kindreds of the nations shall worship before Him. For the kingdom is the Lord's, and He is the Governor among the nations.' These are precious promises; most assuring to all who mourn over the backslidings of men, and think of the millions who are born into this world, and leave it without having heard of a Redeemer. These promises are so boundless and unqualified that faith grows stronger, and hope brighter, as we meditate upon them. Man needs hope as well as faith, to save him from despair, and God has given both, as He ever has given to His children all that is good for them in the varying circumstances of their transitory life. It is impossible for the finite mind to realize all the evil that has sprung since Eve's inclinations developed into a deliberate act of rebellion. But that act and its consequences have fixed on the hearts of men the convictions of the infinite patience of God, who, century after century bears with evil, and overrules it for the sinner's highest and lasting good. Who that has sinned, and suffered, and learned in the experience of suffering to know himself, can fail to realize that, but for the knowledge of evil, he could not have realized what goodness is. The more the sinless life of the Crucified is studied, the clearer all truth becomes. The world, and the world's knowledge, teach us nothing of the mystery of sin and suffering. Christ's life teaches us enough to enable us to *know* that, in the end, greater good to mankind will come through evil, than if evil had not existed. This comes as a clear revelation to a believer in Christ: while the atheist uses the existence of pain and evil as his strongest argument against the existence of God. The cruelty, hypocrisy, reckless waste, selfishness, pride, with their attendant evils, allowed, perpetuated, transmitted from parents to children: the innocent suffering for the guilty: the souls and bodies of one generation after another injured, marred, and distorted by the sins of their forefathers—are proofs to the Atheist of the truth of his theory: and if this world were all, if there were no Incomprehensible, if the atheist's premises were correct, his conclusion, as a reasonable being *using* his reason, is inevitable. Thank God, all false theories are to disappear some day, as mist does before the rising sun.

No pæan was ever raised in a world of sin and death that was so welcome as this, 'Jesus came to seek and to save that which was lost.' Not on earth only was the proclamation made. Straight from the crucified body which Jesus had taken of the ever-blessed Virgin Mary, to offer as a sacrifice for the sins of the whole world, He went 'to preach to the spirits in prison'; to all who had failed by reason of sin to find the 'narrow way' on earth: to those of whom Christ said, 'It shall be more tolerable for Tyre and Sidon at the day of judgment' than for Chorazin and Bethsaida; 'For,' said the Lord, to the cities wherein most of His mighty works were done, 'if the mighty works which were done in you had been done in Tyre and Sidon, they would have repented long ago in sackcloth and ashes.' Those words give us clear spiritual insight of the unseen world. When they were spoken by Christ, He had not been seen in Hades, therefore, 'the light of the knowledge of God as seen in the face of Jesus Christ,' had not shined upon its inhabitants. For long centuries the great majority of the descendants of Adam had been in Hades; and from what St. Peter tells us of Christ, that 'He was put to death in the flesh; but quickened in the spirit' (the human spirit), we have sure ground for believing that when the soul of man enters the spirit-world, there is an increase of spiritual vitality; and with the increase of spiritual vitality, there must be a fuller operation of the Holy Ghost. Hence it follows that the work of the third Person of the Blessed Trinity is not confined to earth, and bound by the measuring line of time; its sphere is the spirit-world, and it is He, who is to abide with us for ever, who builds up and enlightens the spiritual body in which we shall dwell through eternity. There is but one Gospel: and when the Lord Jesus had preached that Gospel on earth, He went to preach the same in Hades; and, bearing in mind that the *flesh* wars against the spirit, can it be doubted that the Lord's teaching in the world of spirits had grander immediate results than His teaching in this world had? 'And thou, Capernaum,' the blessed Saviour said, 'which art exalted unto heaven, shalt be brought down to hell: for if the mighty works which have been done in thee had been done in Sodom, it would have remained until this day. But I say unto you, that it shall be more tolerable for the land of Sodom in the day of judgment, than for thee.' Yes, for justice and mercy are equally balanced by the King of kings, and Capernaum sinned against clearer light than shone upon Sodom. It is written, 'The truth shall make you free,' and when the Son of God entered Hades, He did not go to tell the prisoners that they were lost for ever, and that on the awful day when each one would be punished or rewarded according to the deeds done in the body, the once lost soul would not be received by the Father, when it had become purified through the fiery chastisement of God's wrath against sin. He had just laid down

His life for the sins of the whole world; and He went to Hades to teach the wanderers and the disobedient of earlier days the lessons which He had been teaching on earth; and to tell them of a land of light, and love, and rest from sin, which He had purchased for them; and that He was 'the Way, the Truth, and the Life': the One who had come down from heaven to seek and to save the lost: who had uttered the omnipotent cry from the Cross, 'Father, forgive them, for they know not what they do.' Not till the last man to be saved *is* saved can those words cease to vibrate on the Father's ear: never can they fail to give hope to the sinner; for heaven and earth may pass away, but God's words shall not pass away. Nevertheless, all must stand before the Judgment-throne, each to receive the due reward of His sins; and if for every idle word 'man shall have to give account,' how much sorer punishment awaits those who only did evil continually during their mortal life?

Just as one star differeth from another star in glory; just as every thought, and word, and deed, leaves its impress upon the spirit of man, and, like a good or bad mark in school, has its positive result in determining not only reward or loss of something but the amount of gain or loss—so man's faith and works on earth decide his position in the next stage of existence. 'Whatsoever a man soweth, that shall he also reap.' He sows on earth, as He moves on in the Great Procession towards the border-land, where he is stripped of his working dress, the material substance of his flesh, which he leaves to be buried; while he, in the divinely-fashioned form in which lies his identity, goes to the spirit-world; it may be, to be at peace in 'Abraham's bosom'; it may be to join the disobedient, in the region where remorse, and the recollection of lost opportunities and acts of wilful, unrepented sin, will be his portion of torment; or it may be to join those who are to be beaten with few stripes, because they knew not their Lord's will.

The infinite pity of the Good Shepherd for His lost sheep was manifested when He taught in parables; so that those who could not bear the full light of truth should not see what, if rejected, would increase their condemnation. But when knowledge of the written word of God had kindled light, which, but for wilful blindness, would have enabled man to see in Christ the fulfilment of Messianic prophecy, Jesus said, 'The men of Nineveh shall rise in judgment with this generation, and shall condemn it; because they repented at the preaching of Jonas; and, behold, a greater than Jonas is here.' With what adoring love and gratitude must the men of Nineveh have welcomed Him of whom Jonas was a type! What a wave of light must have flooded Hades, when the 'Light that lighteth every man that cometh into the world' stood among its expectant inhabitants.

And again Christ said, 'The queen of the south shall rise up in judgment with this generation, and shall condemn it: for she came from the uttermost parts of the earth to hear the wisdom of Solomon; and, behold, a greater than Solomon is here.' What would He say to the world now, and to those who, living under the dispensation of the Holy Ghost, close their eyes to the light, and live and act as if spiritual life and spiritual growth were nonentities, and immortality—the long, unending life beyond the grave—were not worth thinking about? The judgment upon such an age has been foreshadowed: 'To whom much is given, of him much will be required.'

An intelligent faith in what is called the 'supernatural' enables man to understand himself and his history; it accounts in a reasonable way for his aspirations towards a better state of things than exists in this world; it gives him a clear apprehension of his origin and of his destiny, of his Creator, and of the union in his own nature of the Divine and human. Weak faith degenerates often into mere superstition. Strong faith with sound reason enable men to soar far above all visionary doubts and mental hallucinations into a region where they attain an absolute knowledge of the fact that man is a superhuman being. That fact opens man's eyes and heart to such an expansive view of Nature and Revelation, that he realizes the universal brotherhood of mankind, and its continuity from the beginning; he regards the 'great procession' as one family. What were sometime mysteries become plain realities; and they who find that day by day the shadows of ignorance are growing less, and the light of wisdom and the power of vision are increasing, scarcely need the reappearance on earth of those who have gone to the world of spirits to assure them of their existence in another sphere. Yet God permits them from time to time to revisit earth. He remembers our many infirmities, and our temptations to unbelief in the unseen, and He vouchsafes to man whatever is needful to confirm his faith in eternal verities. Samuel was permitted to appear to Saul, and, as he had done when in the flesh, he spoke to the king as a prophet sent by God, telling him that, because he had not obeyed the voice of the Lord, the kingdom had been rent from his hand and given to David. The daughter of Jairus was recovered from death. The son of the widow of Nain was restored to his mother. Lazarus entered again that mortal body which had lain four days in the tomb. Tradition says that he was never seen to smile after he was raised from the dead. It may be so, for he was the friend of Jesus, and it is written, 'Blessed are the dead that die in the Lord.' He, like the beggar who lay at the rich man's door, may have been led by angels to a place of rest and light and love; so that earth, henceforth, could have no charm for him. He came back at the bidding of his Lord, and again went about among men, a living monument of the power of God; but—so great is the wilful blindness of fallen man—because his presence at Bethany proved that Jesus of Nazareth was what He claimed to be, God-Incarnate, 'the chief priests consulted that they might put Lazarus to death, because, by reason of him, many of the Jews went away and believed on Jesus.' Well was it said unto them, 'Ye fools, and blind!' as if He who had raised the dead once could not put forth His Almighty power again, and cause Lazarus to witness against their wickedness and hypocrisy if He willed so to do. They who sat in the seat of Moses; who built the tombs of the prophets and garnished the sepulchres of the righteous; who boasted that if they had lived in the days of their fathers, they would not have been partakers with them in the blood of the prophets, were witnesses unto themselves that they *were* the children of them that killed the prophets; for they were even then plotting against Him of Whom the prophets wrote.

What but the supernatural at which the world scoffs; what but the vital force which pervades the universe and sustains all, from the least to the greatest, in the kingdoms of Nature and Grace;

what less powerful than this would account for the fact that the haughty priests and pharisees of Jerusalem stood silent before the despised and rejected Nazarene, when, with the dignity of a judge and the authority of a king, He delivered His withering charge, and declared their condemnation? The day of sacrifice was near, but it had not dawned. The hour when the Saviour of the world would surrender Himself into the hands of His enemies, and permit them to fill up the measure of their iniquity, had not arrived; and until then they could do nothing: for it was God Himself who spoke to them, God manifest in the Person of His Son.

It is an essential dogma of revealed religion that God was from all eternity manifested by His only begotten Son, the Word, who was from the beginning 'in the *Form* of God': and the sacred books of the Old Testament seem to tell us very clearly that that Form or embodiment was in the human shape. Hence it is written that man was made 'in the image of God.' Here, again, a marvellous chord in the universal harmony of creation is struck, and man can but wonder and adore while raising a glad *Te Deum* because he is permitted in this lower sphere to hear the music of heaven, and to feel in his whole being the influence of its vibrations. Thus he learns that the grand scale includes the lower notes on earth as well as the higher ones in heaven. When the invisible creations of God are spiritually discerned, and the reality of the unseen is so impressed upon the mind that the objects of sight and sense do not cloud or efface that impression; when faith by the teaching of the Holy Spirit has become so strong, and reason so elevated and expanded as to be one with faith, man does not say, '*I believe*,' he says, '*I know*,' as did the patriarch Job in old time. Then he sees deeper into the mysteries which surround him, and he is able to connect the seemingly disjointed fragments of sacred and profane history: the teaching of the Holy Spirit shows him how to put them together, as a skilful workman combines his kaleidoscopic materials so as to form a beautiful mosaic; and in the light which is given without measure to those who have the 'willing mind,' the fact gradually becomes clear that with God there is no mystery, and for us it is simply something that we cannot at present understand. We must, however, still use the term which our limitation of knowledge requires. The harmony of creation we may reverently call 'God's masterpiece.' With it revelation begins and note by note is added, until at the close there is the grand 'Amen.' It is a harmony that gladdens the hearts of all who can hear it as they go forward in the great procession; and the more they study the various parts the more perfect the harmony is found to be. It is written, 'Thou canst not see My face; for there shall no man see

Me, and live.' 'No man hath seen God at any time ; the only begotten Son, which is in the bosom of the Father, He hath declared Him.' It is the Lord Jesus Christ who at His appearing shall show ' Who is the blessed and only Potentate, the King of kings, and Lord of lords ; Who only hath immortality, dwelling in the light which no man can approach unto ; Whom no man hath seen, nor can see.' Hence we know that when, in the Old Testament, it is said that the Lord appeared and talked with men, it was the second Person of the Holy Trinity who caused Himself to become visible to mortals ; and that it was in the form of man He communed with Abraham, wrestled with Jacob, and blessed him, and stood before Joshua 'as the Prince of the host of the Lord.' He did *eat* before Abraham ; He *touched* Jacob ; He came as the Captain of an army to encourage and strengthen Joshua. We feel that we are approaching holy ground as we meditate upon these records ; nevertheless, they were 'written for our learning,' and if we fail to study them and gather from them all that they were intended to teach us, we must suffer loss.

It would seem that the Son of God, who is the 'express image of the Father,' the 'brightness of His glory,' and existing in 'the *form* of God,' was also the model of God's last creation, man ; for it is said, 'Let us make man in our image.' The organism of the Divine Son was in some unique manner, even then, the same as man's organism—the same though under different conditions. This seems to have been confirmed when the risen Lord appeared to His disciples and said unto them, 'Peace be unto you.' 'But they were terrified and affrighted, and supposed that they had seen a spirit. And He said unto them, Why are ye troubled? and why do thoughts arise in your hearts? Behold My hands and My feet, that it is I Myself: handle Me, and see; for a spirit hath not flesh and bones, as ye see Me have. And when He had thus spoken He showed them His hands and His feet. And while they yet believed not for joy, and wondered, He said unto them, Have ye here any meat? And they gave him a piece of a broiled fish, and of an honeycomb. And He took it, and did eat before them.' At the institution of the Lord's Supper, when Jesus took the cup and gave it to His disciples, saying, 'Drink ye all of it: for this is My blood of the New Testament, which is shed for many for the remission of sins,' He added, 'But I say unto you, I will not drink henceforth of this fruit of the vine until that day when I drink it new with you in my Father's kingdom.' Three distinct epochs of our Lord's life are here referred to: (1) Before His Incarnation: (2) After His Incarnation and Resurrection: (3) After His Ascension and the Resurrection of the faithful. In each epoch the Lord is in the form of man. When He became incarnate He added to that form the material substance of the flesh. After the Crucifixion He went to Hades, leaving His mortal body in the tomb. On the third day He returned to earth, entered the sepulchre where that body had been laid, changed it—even as we are told that those who are alive at His second coming will be changed—and went forth in His resurrection body as the Saviour of the world and the Victor of death.

In that holy sepulchre we are reminded that the Son of God took unto Him, to make His own for ever, something that He had not when He appeared to the patriarchs, something that He had not when he preached to the spirits in prison; for when *He* was in Hades, the crucified body was in the tomb, and guarded by soldiers. When the stone was rolled away from the mouth of the sepulchre, the body had disappeared. May not this *something* be the 'wedding garment' in which all must be clothed who sit down at the marriage supper of the Lamb? It would seem so, for we are told that 'when He shall appear we shall be like Him'; and that before He left His disciples, He said unto them, 'I go to prepare a place for you.' It was the Bridegroom preparing for His bride; and He had prayed the Father that the bride for whose sake He had fought with the powers of darkness, and conquered, might be one with Him, even as He was one with the Father. It was man's entire being that He came to save; and the essential oneness of God and man which is thus proved may be beyond the power of reason to comprehend, but it is not contrary to it. This union of things seen and unseen is made manifest in a remarkable degree by the fact, that in each of the three epochs of Christ's life, He is represented as *eating* material things as mortal man does. When we know even as we are known, we shall see how, in God's laboratory, Nature's laws reorganize, and assimilate, and mould all things according to the unchanging will of the Lawmaker. It is as illogical to disbelieve what we cannot understand, as it would be to deny the existence of things that we have never seen. Words utterly fail, and thought, though limitless in its capacity, fails too, when we try to grasp all the harmony involved in the revealed facts—the fringe of which is but touched here—of the three epochs of the life of the Son of God; but the key-note of the wondrous harmony is the absolute oneness of God and man in Christ.

In respect of man's state in the future, it has been clearly revealed that he is to live as man through eternity; and when restored to the Divine image in which he was created, he will fulfil his destiny by perfectly doing his Father's will. If men only realized in part what they are, sin would not be allowed to reign in their mortal bodies. The glorious harmony of God's dealings with His children would kindle a desire to live better lives than most men and women dream of now. They would feel that time is not given to be wasted; that man is not born into the world to live for himself alone, nor for the world alone, for his life is divided into two—a life in time, and a life in eternity, the former being a preparation for the latter. If he choose evil, and refuse to walk uprightly, he must suffer loss; for 'what a man sows, he must also reap.'

The Scripture says, 'Cast thy bread upon the waters, and thou shalt find it after many days.' It is only at the end of the 'many days' that the result of casting the bread upon the waters will be known; and the man of God is content to work and wait. He knows that a few kind words spoken to a fellow-traveller may be as leaves from the tree of life; and that a kind deed done heartily, as unto the Lord, changes the feet and hands of man into instruments of God's own handiwork. So powerful is man, and so great is his dignity, that he should never ask, What *can* I do? but, What *may* I do? for what a man of willing mind *can* do for God in this life is, in one sense, illimitable. A good man's ways are ordered by the Lord. He distributes to every man severally as He will; He gives the time, and the opportunity, and the talents to each, for the work which He expects each to do; and life's work well done always ends in victory. To the hardy sons of toil, as to the rulers of kingdoms, the 'Well done, good and faithful servant!' will be the greeting of the King of kings. The Angel of Death, though he seem to slay, only strikes off the fetters that bind man to earth until his present task is accomplished, or the time allowed for doing it has expired.

Not until the veil of mortality is rent, and the spirit of man is set free, can he see clearly how those things which seemed to be most against him were working together for his good—not a mere transitory good that ends when the last grain of sand in Time's hour-glass has fallen, but the good that lives and grows through eternity. When Nature lies sleeping beneath the snow, she is gathering up strength for the time when the decree of the Spring-breath shall say, 'Let the earth bring forth.' Then earth awakes from her wintry slumber to fulfil her mission; and in her summer beauty, and her autumn glory, gives to man her fragrance and her fruits. Even so it is that when some great sorrow comes to us, and chills and blights our life, we lie down beneath its shadow; and in the cold and the darkness we rest, lonely and sad, our eyes and hearts alike closed to the small cares and worries of life, which so often, like a moth fretting the ermine, destroy the beauty of that which, if let alone and hidden for a time, would come forth unharmed like gold from the crucible. And all the while we are preparing for the work which follows the long rest—for the day that comes after night, for the life that follows the great final change which takes place as each member of the great procession passes out of sight. That change seems sudden, but it is only the end of the school-term, when each has to realize how much he has lost or gained by using aright, or misusing, the time and talents bestowed upon him. A grand career along a path of light, in the world to come, is the portion of that man who, here below, has proved himself a hero in the path of duty—the man who, whether in great things or small, has scorned 'to do less than his utmost, or to be less than his best.' '*L'ouvrage des hommes sur la terre ne se mesure pas à la quantité de leurs forces physiques, mais à la quantité de leur volonté.*' The noblest natures, by gradually forgetting self in the pursuit of holiness, or in labouring for the good of others, make unconsciously the greatest sacrifice man can make. It is a sacrifice which is acceptable to God, for it is God-like in its nature. 'My son, give me thine heart,' is the call; and when that call is answered by the surrender of self, man has done all he can do, and the Blood of Jesus washes away all dust of earth that may cling to him, and the hero is brought into the presence of the King, pure and holy, without spot or wrinkle. Such men 'sow in tears,' for, as has been truly said, 'suffering is an inevitable part of the training of those who are to carry God's choicest gifts of consolation to others;' but, 'they reap in joy,' and 'service wrought for God and His people is not arrested, not suspended by death, only transferred elsewhere; only raised to a truer, higher sphere, where the chill of disappointment and the check of error can never come.'

As the mind tries to imagine the 'great procession,' and to learn some lessons from the lives of individual soldiers as they march in their several companies, we cannot fail to observe that the best soldiers of the Cross are the hardest workers, and the most untiring helpers of their fellow-men; consequently they are the most Christ-like in their lives. Having fought the good fight, and finished their course, the joy of youth comes back to them in their old age, and the peace which the world can neither give nor take away is the portion of all who, nearly at the end of a long day's march, find themselves in the 'narrow path,' 'so far from the childhood which is transitory, yet so near to that which is eternal.'

I once saw a portrait. It was of a young man; the prevailing expression was, I think, that of calm gentleness. There were other characteristics, but of those I need not write. About the same time that I saw the portrait, I saw the original of the portrait. He was *then* past the prime of life, but full of energy, allowing himself no time for folding his arms, and looking on, while those who were under his command, and walked with him in the procession, did the work for the Lord that was needed. Often, indeed, he worked harder than they did in that part of the vineyard through which they were passing. He was then a Bishop of the Church. The face was bronzed, and the skin had lost the smoothness of youth. The weight of the pastoral staff might then have begun to tell upon his strength. The responsibility of office, the care of the flock committed to his charge, and his mental and physical labour had left their impress upon the man. Careworn, was the verdict which the face proclaimed. The portrait of the young man was no longer a likeness of the Bishop; I could see but a faint resemblance, even when, in friendly intercourse, the weight of care was lightened for a passing hour. Many years passed away, and again I met the Bishop. The King had called His servant to cease from his work, and to rest awhile ere he passed on home. A quiet waiting-time had come for the aged Bishop, and while thus waiting he seemed to have grown young again. The old face was lighted up by the spirit that never grows old; the lines which time had marked and toil had deepened were softened, and the man of four-score years and ten wore again the look which the artist had caught and depicted on the canvas so many years before. So it is in the kingdom of

God. The morning and the evening are one day, and in its light the young and the old meet, and are seen to be one in spirit and in destiny. The Lord has said, 'All shall know Me, from the least unto the greatest'; and at the close of man's journey upon earth, whether he be old or young, the knowledge of the one God stamps each with the same likeness. Just as in the home-circle, the features and character of the parents are discernible in the children, so in God's children may be traced, amidst endless diversity, the likeness to their great Father; the likeness impressed by Faith upon all who from the beginning of time have walked with God.

Faith in God and immortality causes man to look upward and onward; and as the long procession continues to move on, we see in the steadfast, upward glance, and the unfaltering steps of some of the pilgrims, that they are striving to obtain some great prize; it may be a crown of exceeding glory, which can only be won by taking up, and bearing patiently and bravely, and in the spirit of a little child, a heavy cross; or, it may be a place of light within one of the innermost circles that surround the throne of the Eternal; and perhaps that height can only be attained—by some who are 'running the race'—by means of that strong faith which is, as it were, born of darkness; the darkness caused by intense light, as when the natural eye is blinded for a time by gazing at the sun.

CHAPTER IV.

THE GREAT KINGDOM.

HISTORY tells of the rise and fall of nations; of the might and power and dominion of victorious kings. Ruined cities testify to the wealth and the magnificence of the people who once inhabited them; temples which, even in decay, excite the wonder of men in modern times, by their stupendous grandeur, are monuments, not merely of lofty conceptions and of practical ability, but also of the devotion of past generations. At the root of even the grossest forms of idolatry, there ever has been a 'feeling after God,' which does but find a misguided expression in idol worship. Belief in God is essential to man's very being. He may deny the fact that there is a God; he may even persuade himself that he believes there is no God: but the persuasion is a delusion, for the impression of a primal source of being belongs to his very nature. He may try to destroy the 'image' in which he was made, by heaping doubt upon doubt, and sin upon sin, but he cannot succeed, for 'God is love,' and has a desire to the work of His own hand. God is powerful, man is weak, and the weak must fall before the strong. Man may mar, and almost deface, the God-like image that is in him, but as long as there is life it may be said to him :

> 'You may break, you may ruin the vase if you will,
> But the scent of the roses will hang round it still.'

Belief in God, taking one form or another, is inseparable from man. We know but little here below, yet who will venture to say that when the Red Indian raises his eyes to the sky above him, and gives the first whiff of his pipe to the 'Great Spirit,' *that* act of worship is not accepted by the one and only God? And not only accepted, but recorded in the Book of Life, as a loving offering from one to whom little had been given on earth.

The kingdoms of the old world have passed away, and their kings have gone the way of all flesh. So will it be with the kingdoms and their rulers of to-day. But there is a kingdom which is not *of* this world, although it is *in* this world, of which there will be no end, since it is an 'everlasting kingdom'; and the glorious majesty of that kingdom shall not pass away. It is the kingdom of the Lord God Almighty, who is Governor among the nations; the King of kings, and Lord of lords; the blessed and only Potentate, by whom earthly monarchs reign; who upholdeth all things by the word of His power.

He who said, 'By Me kings reign,' also said, 'I, if I be lifted up from the earth, will draw all men unto me.' Those blessed words were spoken by human lips; the same lips from which afterwards came the seven last sayings of Jesus on the cross. The cross was set up among the kingdoms of the world, by order of the rulers of earthly power. He who gave Himself as a Sacrifice for the sins of the whole world, died upon it the death of a malefactor. That Sacrifice was, as it were, the cornerstone of the new spiritual kingdom. It seemed to be laid in weakness; but St. John tells of a great 'silence in heaven,' and of seven angels, to whom trumpets were given, standing before God, prepared to sound. And after the six angels had sounded, another mighty angel came down from heaven, who stood upon the sea and upon the earth, and lifting up his hand to heaven, 'he sware by Him who liveth for ever and ever, who created heaven and the things that therein are, and the earth, and the things that therein are, and the sea, and the things that are therein, that there should be time no longer: but in the day of the voice of the seventh angel, when he shall begin to sound, the mystery of God should be finished, as He hath declared to His servants the prophets.' 'And,' St. John writes, 'when the seventh angel sounded there were great voices in heaven, saying, The kingdoms of this world are become the kingdom of our Lord, and of His Christ; and He shall reign for ever and ever.'

We have here set before us the result of the sowing and the reaping—the day of seemingly small things on earth, and the triumphant song of victory in heaven, because the Victim of Calvary had crowned His finished work by delivering up the kingdom which He had won to the Father.

'The God of Our Lord Jesus, the Father of Glory,' set the Son of Mary, after His glorious resurrection and ascension, 'at His own right hand in the heavenly places, far above all principality, and power, and might, and dominion, and every name that is named, not only in this world, but also in that which is to come; and put all things under His feet, and gave Him to be Head over all things to the Church: which is His body, the fulness of Him that filleth all in all.' There, in His glorified humanity, the God-Man is seated as King, 'For He must reign till He hath put all enemies under His feet.' 'And when all things shall be subdued unto Him, then shall the Son also Himself' (as the Son of Mary) 'be subject unto Him who put all things under Him, that God,' the One Triune Lord of the universe, 'may be all in all.' And the children of Christ's kingdom, made like unto their Redeemer by the work of the Holy Spirit in them, and having obtained an entrance into the everlasting kingdom, shall be one with Christ for ever, even as the Father, the Son, and the Holy Ghost are One.

Jesus sealed the work of Redemption by uttering the words 'It is finished.' After His resurrection He ceased to be seen by the world, though He remained for awhile on the earth, and showed Himself as a 'perfect God and perfect Man,' to those who should be heirs of the kingdom which He was about to found. Veiled in His changed body, the King of Glory tarried upon earth to lay the foundations of His kingdom which, like Himself, was to be spiritual and universal, and to last for ever. Henceforth His kingdom, was to be *visible* under the form of an organized body, which is known as the Church; and during the forty days between His resurrection and ascension, we are told that He was instructing His disciples concerning the kingdom.

As the temple of Solomon, 'when it was in building,' was built of stones made ready before they were brought thither, so that there was neither hammer nor axe, nor any tool of iron heard in the house while it was in building, so the Church of Christ was begun in silence. Living stones were chosen for the foundation of the great sacramental edifice, which, St. Paul tells us, was to be built upon the foundation of the apostles and prophets, Jesus Christ Himself being the chief Corner-Stone. The stones were taken from the common quarry : they were lightly esteemed, and of no value in the eyes of the world. Many of them were rough-hewn stones : there was no beauty in them to be desired, and they were despised and rejected, even as the Corner-Stone was rejected. Had the great ones of the earth been told that the living energy pervading those stones was omnipotent, and that upon those unpolished and seemingly insignificant stones a mighty edifice would be built, against which the united power of men and spirits could not prevail; that every weapon forged against it would be powerless to overthrow it—they would have laughed the prophet to scorn. The haughty Roman, once master of the world, enthroned in pomp and power in his seven-hilled city, little thought that the time was not far distant when the pride of the Pagan would be laid low, and his gods cast down to make room for the Cross. The Emperor and the senate at Rome knew nothing of what was passing in Jerusalem ; and if they had known we may be sure that the scenes in the Upper Chamber, in Pilate's Judgment Hall, and round the Cross of Calvary, would have been of no interest to them ; even as to the world now, they are nothing more than events of the past, remembered by many for reasons which the world does not care to dwell upon, or try to understand. And why is it so? When the longest life is so short, when man knows that he must die, and leave everything behind him, why does he not care to learn something of the *spirit-world*, something of the *future life*, something of the *purpose* of the present life? It must be because the world with which he has cast in his lot is spiritually dead.

Every man knows that 'It is appointed unto men once to die; nay, more, that death is the most certain of all events; and yet the majority of human beings live as if there were no such thing to fear. They live as if the social, moral, and political state of the world would go on for ever as it does now, and as it has done through former ages. They never give themselves time to think of or to learn aught concerning the spiritual part of their being, and concerning the life beyond the grave; and so they do not realize that what belongs only to the material world must come to an end. It has always been so. Were not the men and women of old time doing just as men and women do now, when the flood came and swept them away from the face of the earth? Did Lucifer, when, as a 'son of the morning,' he first conceived sin and in the pride of his heart said, ' I will ascend into heaven, I will exalt my throne above the stars of God. I will ascend above the heights of the clouds: I will be like the Most High'; did he think that he should be brought down to hell? Did the inhabitants of Capernaum in the exaltation of their pride think that all they valued would vanish like a dream? Did the Pharaohs of Egypt, and the monarchs of Persia, ever surmise that all their regal power and glory would pass away? Did imperial Rome ever dream that her empire would crumble into dust? Did the ancient nobility of France believe that their brilliant, butterfly life would end in the Reign of Terror? Does Britannia, who 'rules the waves,' ever think that the time will come when her flag which 'has braved a thousand years the battle and the breeze' will be lowered, because the hour has come when, by reason of the inevitable changes of a changing world, and the flight of time, she must take her place among the shades of departed glory? Does England realize that her vast empire, on which, it is proudly said, 'the sun never sets,' must in the natural order of things share the same fate as other empires; that her sun must set, her power must wane, her strength must change to weakness, and her world-wide fame become a thing of the past? Do her rulers realize any more than the Pharaohs and the Cæsars did that their place as kings among men, and their glory as stars of the first or second magnitude in the illimitable universe throughout eternity, depend not upon their material power and grandeur, but upon the *use* they make of the wealth, and the talents, and the opportunities that are bestowed upon them?

All this blindness to the transitory character of

the visible world arises from the fact that the world is spiritually dead; and yet as a great preacher* tells us, 'No truth is more clearly revealed to us than this, that spiritual life, whether given us at our first new birth into Christ or renewed after penitence in later years, is the free fresh gift of the Father of spirits, uniting us by His Spirit to His Blessed Son. Nature can no more give us newness of life than a corpse can rise from the dead by its unassisted powers. "That which is born of the flesh is flesh." A sense of prudence, advancing years, the tone of society around us, family influences, may remodel the surface form of our daily habits. But Divine grace alone can turn the inmost being to God; can "raise it from the death of sin to the life of righteousness"; can "clothe it in that new man which after God is created in righteousness and true holiness."' Then the preacher bids us reflect 'on the reality of spiritual death, linked as it often is in one and the same man, as if by a ghastly ligament to the highest animal and mental life. The body is in the full flush of its powers; the mind day by day plays lightly over the surface, or grapples earnestly with the substance of a thousand topics. But the spiritual life is to all intents and purposes dead; and neither boisterous animal spirits nor intellectual fire can galvanize it into life. The spiritual senses do not act: the

* Dr. Liddon, Canon of St. Paul's.

spiritual world is as if it did not exist. The eye of the soul is closed; it sees in spiritual truth only diseased imaginations or needless scruples. Its ears are closed: Christ and His apostles are to it only like any other talkers in the Babel of human tongues. Its mouth is closed: it never speaks to God in prayer or to men in faith and love. Its hands and feet are tightly bandaged in the graveclothes of selfish habit; it cannot rise; it cannot engage in works of benevolence and mercy for the love of God; it must lie on in the darkness and putrefaction of its spiritual tomb; while death, as the Psalmist says, gnaweth upon it. And a great stone has been rolled to the door of its sepulchre—the dead-weight of corrupt and irreligious opinion which bars out from it the light and air of heaven, and makes its prison-house of death secure. How is such a spell and encumbrance of death to be thrown off, if no help, no motive quickening power, come from on high? Even if angels should roll away the stone, how can life itself be restored unless He who is its Lord and Giver shall flash into this dead spirit His own quickening powers, and bid it see and hear and walk and work, and feel and rejoice in its returning life, and go forth to brace its strength and assert its liberty?'

It is this quickening power in the Head that gives life to the members of the body and causes the Church to live on through the ages, shining as a bright light amid encircling darkness. In order to meet the wants of a being like man, composed of spirit and matter, it must needs be that the instrument for the regeneration of humanity should be one in touch with every part of man's being; and it is the knowledge that the Church is a Divine institution, permeated with the life of its Founder, that invests everything connected with her material organization with such importance. The careless Christian little knows what he is doing when he thinks and speaks lightly of the Church; for she is the instrument God has chosen for the regeneration of mankind, and for transforming the children of Adam into the image which they have lost; to make them again children of God and heirs of the kingdom of heaven. If, owing to the circumstances by which we are surrounded, and the extended knowledge of the state of the modern world, it is more difficult for us to maintain the faith of earlier days than it was for our ancestors, seeing that 'materialism,' if it existed to any appreciable extent, was not then the power in the world that it is now; still, the vast dominion of the new kingdom and her impregnable position in the world, is of itself sufficient to attest her Divine origin, and to prove her possession of superhuman power. The extensive outlook which knowledge of what is passing in all parts of the world now gives us, while showing the vast amount of evil which threatens to overwhelm the good, discloses also to us an unseen power that keeps the evil within bounds, so that it cannot really harm those faithful subjects who choose to walk in the light, and be governed by the laws of that kingdom. The spirit of unbelief cannot prevent the man who thinks at all from regarding the Church with wonder, as he must regard the older Church of the Jews. The Jews are a living proof of the fulfilment of prophecy; the sceptic cannot deny their existence, and he can only ignore them and their past and present history. But that is not exactly a logical or scientific mode of solving a difficult problem, and cannot be satisfactory to a reflective and cultured mind. He is in the same dilemma as regards the Church. He knows her history. He knows when, and how, and by whom the new kingdom was set up. He knows that the whole world was arrayed against her at the beginning, and that through successive centuries all that is adverse to her teaching and her laws has been trying to destroy her. He knows also that her members have held their own through times of storm and sunshine; and that the fires of persecution have but purified and strengthened her for the exercise of her influence in every quarter of the globe. He sees that her power is far above that of earthly kings and princes; and at the same time that her subjects are the most loyal supporters of earthly monarchies, and of national law. They see human institutions spring up and fade away; but the Divine institution grows stronger as the ages roll on. Yet the unbeliever in the Divine origin of the kingdom is content to wonder and pass on; but he will have to learn, in another stage of his existence, how much he has lost by neglecting to educate the unseen and spiritual part of his being.

It has been shown in Chapter II., 'The Great Sacrament, God in Nature,' that within all created things there is an unseen Power at work. That Power is the 'Life of the World,' and all creation reveals His Presence. He clothes Himself with light as with a garment: He moves upon the wings of the wind: He orders the courses of the stars, and He feeds the sparrows. All things great and small are cared for by Him; but His delight is with the sons of men, and it is in His dealings with the children of the new kingdom, the members of the Universal Church, that His power and love are fully unveiled. They are revealed to the heart and mind of man in such transcendent forms, that to those who press on towards the mark of their high calling—and in doing so acquire ever-increasing spiritual insight of the invisible things of God—the things that are *seen* assume their true proportions. They see in the changing world of Nature a material witness to God, and to His unchangeable laws. 'The kingdom of grace is His chosen dwelling-place, and there He abides for ever. It is there that man learns to know his Maker; it is there that the child finds his Father; it is there that the bride meets the Bridegroom; and it is there that the pilgrim; weary of wandering in the wilderness, finds rest and peace in the path that leads straight to one of the many mansions which He is preparing for His followers.

When man, on whom the Almighty God bestowed a portion of His own attributes, with the trust of free-will, which rendered him responsible for his thoughts and words, and deeds, chose *evil* rather than good, God had to deal with the consequences of that free-agency which He had Himself conferred upon man. So great has become the power of self-willed evil in man, that nothing short of the sacrifice of the only-begotten Son of God could overmaster it. Hence the glorious achievements in the spiritual world far outweigh those in the natural world, for material things shall 'wax old as doth a garment, and as a vesture they shall be changed'; but man remains man for ever; a never-dying soul clothed with a material body here, and with an answering spiritual body in the world to come. To measure the value of the soul, we have but to meditate on the words, 'What doth it profit a man, if he gain the whole world, and lose his own soul?' and to realize the cost at which alone it could be ransomed.

It is God the Son who reigns over the new kingdom, and also gives life to all those who enter the kingdom, confess Him before men, and obey His laws. The life that each member of the body of Christ receives from the Head is a new life, a supernatural life, altogether different to the natural life of man ; for it is written, 'He that hath the Son of God hath life ; and he that hath not the Son of God hath not life.' That new life is effective for resisting, rooting out, and finally overcoming evil, since it is *Christ Himself* dwelling in us.

In an inconceivable but most real manner He gives Himself to all who will receive Him. He sent the Holy Ghost from the Father to prepare each child who enters the kingdom through the waters of Baptism, for participating in the Blessed Sacrament of the Altar and so receiving Christ. Man, therefore, however cultured and moral he may be; however true his allegiance to the Decalogue may be; and however irreproachable his life may be, as judged from the world's highest ethical standpoint, is not a Christian in the proper sense of that word, unless he receives Christ. 'Except ye eat the flesh of the Son of Man and drink His blood, ye have no life in you. Whoso eateth My flesh and drinketh My blood hath eternal life ; and I will raise him up at the last day. For My flesh is meat indeed, and My blood is drink indeed. He that eateth My flesh and drinketh My blood dwelleth in Me and I in him.' And St. Paul writes, 'I am crucified with Christ, nevertheless I live, yet not I, but Christ liveth in me.' This is not the vitality which Adam had, even before the Fall: The new life is something more mystical than that; it is more than words can tell, or thought conceive. It is enough that Jesus has said, 'I will not leave you comfortless (or orphans), I will come unto you. Yet a little while, and the world seeth Me no more: but ye see Me: because I live, ye shall live also. At that day ye shall know that I am in My Father, and ye in Me, and I in you.'

Again, St. Paul says: 'We are members of His body, of His flesh, and of His bones. For this cause shall a man leave his father and mother, and shall be joined unto his wife, and they two shall be one flesh. This is a great mystery: but I speak concerning Christ and the Church.'

It is difficult for a Christian who has once grasped the full meaning of the teachings of our Lord and of His apostles concerning the union of the Divine and human, 'not by confusion of substance, but by unity of person,' to understand how anyone professing Christianity can fail to see, that it is impossible to exalt the Church higher than her Lord has exalted her; because if we believe the Holy Scriptures to be the inspired Word of God, then Christ and His Church are one, indissolubly and for ever one. The Church cannot be severed from her Head and live. 'I am the Vine, ye are the branches: he that abideth in Me, and I in him, the same bringeth forth much fruit,' for severed from Me, ye can do nothing. But the Church does live; she lives to bear much fruit; she lives to work for her Lord, to uphold His kingdom, to fight for Him against the world, the flesh, and the devil; she lives to suffer, and grow strong in the path of suffering, for the everlasting arms are always stretched out to help and defend her. She lives to conquer and be crowned.

A failure to recognise the fact that Christ and His Church are *one* is doubtless the main cause of prevailing unbelief in the Church as a Divine institution, and in her sacramental character. The god of this world, knowing that the soul can only live in the light of the Sun of Righteousness, is content when he sees the great majority regarding the Church as merely human, and fixing their attention upon her crumbling stones, her tottering walls, her desecrated shrines, her broken altars; traitors among her self-styled members, and the blind, and the deaf, the blasphemer, and the hypocrite within her borders. But this is only one phase of the visible Church; there is another phase, which it would be well for those who deny Divine life in the Church to consider. That phase is her work in the world. Her organization, her power, her influence for good, and her works of mercy are historical facts; and they tell of superhuman power which has ever been guiding and upholding the weak human agencies employed.

It is the Church of Christ that has preserved the

Scriptures, and, as has been said by a true son of the Church, ' Well may she preserve her sacred deposit; for if to her we owe those Scriptures, without those Scriptures she might have forgotten her own origin and inheritance; for therein is contained the charter of her Christian privileges, promises, and duties ; there we read of the Incarnate Word, the great Head of the Church, into whom we were grafted by Baptism, in whom we live by Faith, of whom we partake spiritually by Sacraments, who is our 'Wisdom, and Righteousness, and Sanctification, and Redemption.'

If all the members of the visible Church realized, as they ought to do, what they owe to the Church, in preserving for them all the laws for the government of Christ's kingdom, and all the lessons which Christ taught, they would so love and reverence her, and fight for her, that even in the eyes of an unbelieving and scoffing world, she would be 'terrible as an army with banners.' Eternity will disclose—what Time would fail to unfold—the blessed effect upon the hearts of millions of human beings of the Church's echo through the ages of her Lord's eight Beatitudes, which ever fall upon the ear and heart like dew upon parched ground, and cause joy and gladness to spring up in the soul. Each is a petal of the Rose of Sharon, wafted from the mountain-side to fill the wide world with fragrance, and revive the drooping spirits of men.

Strong contrasts are necessary to enable the mind of man to realize the great gulf that lies between two opposite things, or two opposing forces. The gulf is usually bridged over by varying ways of stating each of those opposites, so that when they meet midway, it is difficult for even an astute and profound thinker, and impossible for a superficial observer, to determine the precise limits of the statements on either side. As they approach each other the settings become less marked in character, more indefinite and uncertain. There is also a commingling of the opposing forces by reason of an existing state of imperfection; but there can be no union of things that are essentially opposed to each other. From first to last light and darkness, good and evil, health and sickness, truth and falsehood are distinct things. Light dispels darkness, and darkness overshadows light: good overcomes evil, and evil allures and prevails over good: health and sickness cannot exist together, neither can truth and falsehood. At the opposite extremes of good and evil there are Christ and Satan, St. John and Judas, the mother of Jesus and Herodias; but between such extremes, the sharp edges which distinguish one from the other are gradually effaced by man. The vanishing point, where good and evil cease to be, is clear in the sight of God; and St. Paul sets forth the positive separation of the two forces when he writes, 'For I know that in me (that is, in my flesh), dwelleth no good thing: for to will is present with me: but how to perform that which is good I find not. For the good that I would, I do not; but the evil which I would not, that I do. Now, if I do that I *would* not, it is no more I that do it, but sin that dwelleth in me. I find then a law, that, when I would do good, evil is present with me. For I delight in the law of God after the inward man: but I see another law in my members, warring against the law of my mind, and bringing me into captivity to the law of sin which is in my members.' As in St. Paul, so in each member of Christ's body, the two great invisible forces confront each other, and war against each other; and the battle goes on as long as this life lasts. Its progress is chronicled in the lives of men and women; in their words and actions, and in the circles in which they move. Well is it for those who, when the Angel of Death touches them, can say with St. Paul, 'I am now ready to be offered, and the time of my departure is at hand. I have fought a good fight, I have finished my course, I have kept the faith: henceforth there is laid up for me a crown of righteousness, which the Lord, the righteous Judge, shall give me at that day: and not to me only, but unto all them also that love His appearing.' This warfare between good and evil cannot end until evil is rooted out of Christ's kingdom utterly and for ever. Until that day arrives the tares and the wheat must grow together. Then, in the time of harvest, the wheat will be garnered for the Lord of the harvest, and the tares will be burned.

Again, the antagonism of good and evil, of the Church and the world, are manifest in the fruits of the cardinal virtue of love, and in its opposite, hate. Christ loved the world, and gave Himself for it. The world hated truth, and crucified the Lord of Truth. St. Stephen bore witness to the truth, and the world stoned him to death. Christ prayed for His murderers, 'Father, forgive them for they know not what they do'; and when His work on earth was accomplished, He entered heaven as the King of Glory. His disciple prayed, 'Lord, lay not this sin to their charge'; and when he had said this, he fell asleep in the light of heaven, for he 'saw the glory of God, and Jesus standing on the right hand of God,' before he left his mortal body. Who can doubt that the first of 'the noble army of martyrs' lives in glory with Him whom he confessed on earth in the last moments of his mortal agony? Who can doubt that the first confessor of the faith, who sealed his confession with his blood, and so won the martyr's crown, is a prince in the hierarchy of heaven, the higher region of the new kingdom which Christ had founded on earth? 'The blood of the martyrs is the seed of the Church'; the path of suffering is the way of the Cross; and if we examine closely the characteristics of the subjects of Christ's kingdom in all ages, from the days of the apostles to the present time, it will be found that they are unchanged. It must be so, because their model is their King, and He has willed that when He shall again appear His disciples shall be like Him. The new life given in baptism, and the free gift of grace ever flowing from its Source to sustain that life, causes them to grow like Him; and the world sees that the children of the kingdom are not like the children of the world. With all their imperfections, their failures, and their backslidings, the higher and unseen Power that is forming their characters and shaping their destiny, takes a visible form in acts of self-denial, in acts of devotion, in works of love and mercy, in heroic courage, in doing the right when it would be more pleasant or profitable to do the wrong; and often in entire self-sacrifice. The children of this world see all this going on around them to-day, as former generations saw the same things; but, in these days of ease and luxury and indifferentism, instead of using the aggressive weapons of the older fanaticism—which had at least the merit of reality—against the order and usage of the higher life, men now do but look on, wonder, or deride, and, as the modern phrase goes, they 'agree to differ.' So the tares and the wheat grow together in the field of this world. The tares far outnumber the ears of corn, so that the Church is ever like a stronghold compassed about and watched by enemies, who point to the disunion of the soldiers who man the walls, to the insubordination and the shortcomings of individual members of the garrison, and to deserters from the Church Army, and they mockingly ask, 'Where is the One Catholic and Apostolic Church of which you boast?' The answer is, Wherever, throughout the whole world, 'the Faith, once for all delivered,' is held—the truth, as it was summed up in the last Œcumenical Council of Nice; wherever the sacraments are administered by duly ordained priests, according to Apostolic rule; and wherever the Word of God is preached in its entirety. The Church, in her material environment, may appear to be weak; the branches of the Vine may seem to have been wrenched from the stock, but they are not really severed from the Vine; they live, and are united invisibly, so as to form one indestructible creation of Almighty God.

England was once called the 'Isle of Saints'; she is now known as the 'workshop of the world.' Has she then no saints left? Yes, we reply, more than in the olden time. Then, the people were few in number, and each holy man who cared for and taught the poor, and gave up his earthly inheritance to erect and endow churches for the glory of God and the benefit of mankind, was known to all. Now things are changed; millions of men and women now occupy the land where, in other days, there were but hundreds; and the labourers in the vineyard are oftentimes only known to their Lord, and to those with whom they work. Many a man and woman, especially during the last half of the present century, has heard repeated to him the cry of Cyprian to the Church of Carthage, 'Rise to your birthright'; and uncounted numbers have arisen from slumber, and in response to the cry have put on the whole armour of God, which is stored up and ever ready for use in the Church. They have gone forth in the path of duty, proving that in all ages, living stones, like unto those which were chosen by Christ for the foundations of His church, are to be found to add to the building. They are polished by the same means, and fitted by the same Master Builder for the place which each is to occupy. The stake, the fire, and the sword, are not the weapons which the world now uses against those members of Christ's body who try to walk in their Master's footprints. Those deadly weapons did their work quickly and well; but the world now thinks them barbarous and cruel, and has substituted slander, contempt, and mockery, which never kill, only keep the victims writhing like a worm upon a hook. Some, alas! have not been strong enough to resist the prolonged torture, and have left the Mother who nursed them. They left the good old ship, which had safely landed so many on the heavenly shore —when she seemed most to need their help— because they vainly dreamed that rest and peace might be found elsewhere.

> 'They saw the ship by many a tempest toss'd,
> Her rudder broken and her tackling lost;
> Left her to sink without their helping hand,
> Looked to themselves, and basely 'scaped to land.'

They did so to their own great loss, for in the tempest-tossed vessel which they left God Himself had placed them. True to their Captain, and loving the old ship all the more because she seemed to be in danger of losing more than had already been taken from her, others have remained faithful, echoing the words of one who himself fought a good fight :

> 'But shall I, too, the sinking ship forsake?
> Forbid, it, Heaven, or take my spirit back!
> No, ye diviners sage ; your hope is vain.
> While but one fragment of our ship remain,
> That single fragment shall my soul sustain :
> Bound to that sacred plank, my soul defies
> The great abyss, and dares all hell to rise,
> Assured that Christ *on that* shall bear me to the skies.'*

Since those words were first written, the old ship has been righting herself; trimming her sails, strengthening her bulwarks, opening her port-holes, so that the sunlight of heaven, and the fresh, life-

* Charles Wesley.

giving breezes of the ocean of truth may penetrate to the innermost recesses, and purify and strengthen her for the work she has to do. That work is harder, and higher, and nobler than the world can understand, or than most of her own sons and daughters realize. It is co-extensive with God's purpose, and man's necessities.

Has God given to England, or allowed her to acquire and annex the vast empire over which she now rules, *only* in order that she may increase her worldly power and glory? Has He permitted her to extend her sway east, west, north, and south, merely that her fleet may ride at anchor, with England's flag flying at the mast-head, in all seas, and her merchants trade unmolested with all lands, only to enrich themselves and their country? Has God permitted the Imperial crown of India to be placed upon the head of the sovereign of England simply to make that monarch's name a greater power among the millions of Orientals over whom she reigns, and to set, as it were, the seal upon the conquest of India? Not for these things has the King of kings given such world-wide power to England! Not for the accomplishment of these transitory objects, save as means to an end, has He given to the Anglo-Saxon race their keen insight, their love of knowledge, their dogged perseverance, their indomitable courage, their love of freedom and adventure, their marked aptitude for adapting themselves to surrounding circumstances and varying climates, their physical strength, and their power of endurance. Well may St. Cyprian's cry, 'Rise to your birthright,' be proclaimed by the Church, and by the senate, as the paramount duty of every Anglo-Saxon. The Ruler of kings and nations seems to have put England, with her Church and people, in a position like that in which Pharaoh placed Joseph, when he decreed, 'Only in the throne will I be greater than thou.' No human power could uphold and bind together the British Empire, even for a day; for human power is weakness, unless it has with it that superhuman spiritual life which only the Divine Being can impart to man. 'Rise to your birthright' means, Man, learn to know thyself, to understand (1) who and what you are; (2) what you have to do, and to whom you are accountable; (3) to 'quit you like men.' The world needs you. God has set work before you, and He has given dominion, and power, and opportunity, and means to accomplish that work. Do it well and thoroughly for the Master's sake. As surely as man turns a deaf ear to that cry will the sentence of the Judge be pronounced, 'Thou art weighed in the balances and found wanting,' and then England's power will wane, and her empire be broken into fragments.

To every human being the words 'Give an account of thy stewardship' will one day be spoken;

and when it is remembered that to whom much is given of them much will be required, each subject of the British empire who realizes, in however small a degree, his individual responsibility and influence may well tremble at the thought, that the Omnipresent One will measure his work with the infinite line of His justice, will scan his motives and weigh his capabilities, means, and opportunities. Men should pause in their career to ask themselves, Am I doing the work assigned to *me?* Am I doing my *best?* What use am I making of my brains and hands? Am I occupying the time given to me, or am I letting it slip by, moment after moment, hour after hour, day after day, with no record that will bear the light of day or stand the test of judgment? If, as the light of the sun faded daily in the west, each man and woman would ask the question, 'What have I done this day for Him who made me and redeemed me, and who gave me all I have that is worth having?' what would be the reply, even in the case of many professing Christians?

Man cannot rise to his birthright privileges until he ceases to regard himself as a separate being from God. As long as he chooses to consider himself an irresponsible unit, and to believe that he has a perfect right to live for himself alone, and to do what he pleases, physically, morally, and intellectually, without regard to the effect of his life upon others, he cannot understand what his birthright privileges are, and therefore he readily enough casts the claim from him. If he be one of those who are endowed with great mental and physical gifts—with the wealth and rank which give him more than ordinary influence, he, of necessity, in casting the claim aside, reduces himself to a lower level than that which those not so gifted occupy in the sight of the just Judge. Someone has truly said, 'We are nearer to wisdom when we stoop than when we soar,' for there is real greatness in true humility and much littleness in self-assumption. The former is not appreciated by the world; the latter generally makes headway; yet the force underlying humility always exercises—unconsciously to its possessor—great and lasting influence, whereas the spirit of egoism passes along its self-chosen path with a flourish of trumpets, little thinking that the noise, and those who make it, will soon be forgotten.

More than eighteen centuries ago it was said to the Athenians by St. Paul, 'God hath appointed a day in which he will judge the world in righteousness by that man whom he hath ordained, whereof he hath given assurance unto all men in that he hath raised him from the dead.' The Church year by year repeats the solemn words to the men and women of this generation; and tells them that when 'the Son of Man shall come in His glory, and all His holy angels with Him ; and shall sit on the throne of His glory, and before Him shall be gathered all nations,' each individual of the human race must give an account of his stewardship. Then the faithful stewards will receive the due reward of their labours, and the unfaithful will be punished for leaving undone what they ought to have done. Bearing in mind the inevitable effect for good or evil which the life of every man exercises on those around him—just as a pure or impure atmosphere affects the material body—the influence that the rulers of the British empire must exert in the world approximates to the infinite : and the position of England, her Church, her people, and her language, involves so vast a stewardship that even an imperfect realization of the responsibility attaching to it would overwhelm the mind, were it not for the fact which is revealed by God, and proved by history, that in all ages when the Almighty has given some man or nation a great and seemingly impossible work to do He has always said in effect, 'Obey ; go forward ; I will be with you.' 'My grace is sufficient for you.' Who that has a spark of true manliness in him could read that touching appeal of the Creator to His people in the earlier days, 'What could have been done more to My vineyard, that I have not done in it?' and fail to realize that God might say those very words to England at the present day ? And if He should add, 'Give an account of thy stewardship,' what could England answer? She has taken possession of other lands, and peopled them with her own sons and daughters. She has introduced European civilization, and with it the peculiar vices of civilization; but what, as a nation, has she done for the original inhabitants of the territories that have been added to her empire? She has constituted herself guardian of India, and has acquired untold wealth and power in the East by her self-imposed protectorate of that enormous country; but has she made one single *national* effort to reach the *heart* of India, to get in touch with the susceptible nature of Orientals? If, since England became guardian of India, she had taken means to learn more of India's past history; if she had gathered all of truth and all that is Christ-like in the various forms of religion that prevail in that land, and had shown the people that the English believed virtually the same truths, India might now be all our own in the truest sense of the word. India owns the sway of the British sceptre because it is her interest to do so, and because she prospers under English rule; but, except in a worldly sense, India and England are strangers still. There is at present no lasting bond of union, for the chains that link them together are forged by interest and expediency.

 Christ came into this world, and, as man, prepared Himself during thirty years to be a Teacher of men, and then stood forth alone proclaiming Himself to be 'the Way, the Truth, and the Life'; and so men of Christ-like minds have left home and country, and, in the strength of Christ, have gone forth alone to distant lands and have done what they could: and their testimony has converted foes into friends, and aliens in blood, heart and creed, into brothers, and made them heirs of the same kingdom. What Christian can look upon the late venerable Negro Bishop of Africa and read the story of his life without feeling that in Christ all men are brothers?

England's glory is her Church; the strength of England, and the palladium of her ancient monarchy, is the Church. The truest sons and daughters of the Church know that it is so; for, as members of Christ's body, they must be loyal to their Head; and they know it is by Him kings reign. He setteth up one and putteth down another. Therefore they are ever the truest patriots. When anarchy and rebellion threaten, their cry 'For King and Country' is always heard, and rarely, perhaps *never*, do they fail in their loyalty, unless they are ordered to do that which they believe to be contrary to the will of the King of kings. 'Render unto Cæsar the things that are Cæsar's; and unto God the things that are God's.' Individually, the hardest workers in the Lord's vineyard do what they can to advance the new kingdom and bring wanderers into the fold. The Holy Spirit calls them to rise up, and go to some distant spot where the people are still in darkness; or into the far darker places of great cities, where into the most loathsome dens of infamy no ray of light has penetrated—except, perhaps, a flickering one from the window of a gorgeous gin-palace hard by—and they go. Still this is but the power of individuals, and, as such, it is necessarily circumscribed in its sphere. England, as a nation, has not risen to her birthright. The Church sends out her priests and bishops to do their appointed work; but England does not stretch forth her arm of power to protect the uncivilized races of the lands she has made her own, against vices of which the aborigines knew nothing until the white man came. The Church will, we know, conquer in the end; but woe to the nation that hinders her work by not supporting her with its might.

The world would, of course, scoff at the idea of the Church being the strength of England; but that the idea is not a phantom but a great reality is easily proved. Granted, for the sake of argument, that the Church is *only* a human institution; since that is the only ground on which an unbeliever in its Divine origin can stand. At the outset he would find himself face to face with incontestable facts. This is one—the Church is a Teacher. She inculcates obedience to law and order and to all who are in authority. She directs subjects to submit themselves to the ruler who is set over them, teaches children to be obedient to their parents, servants to obey their masters, 'not with eye-service as men-pleasers, but in singleness of heart, fearing God.' She enforces on men the necessity of obeying the Decalogue. She builds schools for training the young, because she believes in Him who has said, 'Train up a child in the way he should go, and when he is old he will not depart from it.' She builds alms-houses for sheltering the aged poor, refuges for the penitent, asylums for the blind and the deaf and dumb; hospitals for the sick; in short, she, as a whole, working in and by her members, maintains the whole social status of England on its present level. The sovereign of England has a solemn oath to take before the crown can be worn, or the sceptre held. Blot out that oath; cast away the ancient ceremony of the coronation as useless and unmeaning—which it is if the sovereign is not responsible and accountable to a higher authority; remove the archbishops and bishops from their thrones as being self-appointed authorities, and claimants of power which does not belong to them. Level every cathedral and church to the ground, and turn all Church institutions into places of amusement. Banish every member of the Church who is teaching, nursing, and helping the poor, and send out of the country

THE GREAT KINGDOM

with them all those who, by their means, have been turned out of the path of evil into a better way. Destroy every vestige of Church art wherever it may be found, from the masterpieces of Raphael and Murillo to the engraving of the 'Good Shepherd.' Suppress every note of music that has a Church ring in it, from Handel's 'Messiah' to Sullivan's 'Lost Chord.' Sweep away every poem that treats of immortality and of the higher life of man in Christ; and all literature that teaches man what he is, or ought to be, and what he may be. Strike at the root of every aspiration beyond the region of materialism. Sap the foundations of belief in the holy Catholic Church; the personality and teaching of the Holy Ghost; the communion of saints; the forgiveness of sins; the resurrection of the body, and the life everlasting. Do all this and what will be left? What would England be if it were robbed of all these things?

Let every cultured unbeliever honestly face that question. He would be a bold man who would venture to assert that the island-home of which Englishmen are so proud would be other than a pandemonium. And, with all else that the Church has given, hope would depart; yet without hope what is life worth? The man who is without faith and hope cannot rise above the dead level indicated by the words, 'Let us eat and drink, for tomorrow we die.' Compared with such as these to what a height had the noble Hebrew woman, mentioned in the Second Book of Maccabees, attained when she exhorted her seven sons in turn to resist the commands of a profane tyrant. She knew nothing of the glorious revelation of our Lord Jesus Christ, nor the power of His resurrection; but the faith of the Father of the faithful enabled her to say, as each of her sons went forth to his martyrdom, 'I know not how you were formed in my womb; for I neither gave you breath, nor soul, nor life, neither did I frame the limbs of every one of you; but the Creator of the world, that formed the nativity of man, that found out the origin of all, He will restore to you again in His mercy both breath and life.'

If the work of the visible Church can accomplish so much that even her enemies are constrained to admit that practically they could not 'get on' without her, and that *somehow* her influence helps them to keep the existing conditions of life from getting worse than they are, is it not marvellous that men of deep learning and acute observation do not try to solve the problem: 'How has the Church come to acquire the power which has established her in the world; which sustains her, and causes her to grow wherever she is planted, even in the midst of adverse elements; which has given her such a mighty empire over the minds of men, over minds of profound depth, expansive tendencies, and intellectual faculties of the highest order?' In science men have to work backward. They have fact before them, and that is, necessarily, the starting-point; as, for instance, in the force of gravitation: its effect and ultimate result led to a knowledge and study of the law. In the case of that kingdom which is in the world, but not of it; the kingdom which is to be universal and everlasting—in other words, the Church of God—it is different. Man may commence his study of the question with the Founder, or work backward to Him. The result will be the same; there is clear, historical evidence that all the good which Christianity has brought to mankind flows from its Source—the Man who was crucified on Mount Calvary. The men of that day, who knew not what they were doing, mocked at and passed by the Cross, as those who follow in their footprints do to-day; for the centuries that have rolled between what was then and what is now have not changed the heart of man. The Church militant, though a mighty power in the world, is no more to that proud world than the Son of God was to the blind, Pharisaical Jews and the haughty Romans, when He went from city to city doing good and reproving vice. 'As with the Head, so with the members.' The sun of the Christian system set to the world when the last words of the Saviour, 'Father, into Thy hands I commend My spirit,' were uttered. It rose again, unseen by the world, on the third day; but the infant Church saw it, and believed in its eternal glory. In all succeeding ages her children have manifested their faith by their works. They have laboured, and fought, and died for her; for her divine life is also their life. They live here below as pilgrims seeking a better country, and when they seem to die they do but close their mortal eyes, to open the eyes of the soul in their true home. Here they have to 'wrestle against principalities, against powers, against the rulers of the darkness of this world, against spiritual wickedness in high places, against the prince of the power of the air.' Wordsworth says (in note on Eph. ii. 2), 'Satan and his angels being cast down from heaven, but not being yet consigned to hell, have their empire in this lower air, and are therefore called powers of the air and of darkness.' And St. Jerome says, 'It is the opinion of all the Doctors of the Church that the intervening air between heaven and earth is full of adverse powers.'

The experience of God's children in every age—not excepting the present age of reason—bears testimony to the truth of Revelation on this subject. Who is free from evil thoughts, which come suddenly from without, as if whispered in the ear, when the mind is intent upon other things; sometimes they come in horrible dreams, when, perhaps, the last waking thought of the sleeper was embodied in the words, 'Father, into Thy hands I commend my spirit.' Who has not sometimes felt tempted to do the very thing he would not do, and which his soul abhors? The devil tempted Christ and failed; he and his angels tempt man, and too often succeed. God's greatest saints are often the most sorely tempted, as in the case of the patriarch Job; but God and His angels of light are looking on, and when faith has been tried, when suffering has done its work, when the fire has purified the gold, then one of those ministering spirits sent forth to minister to them who shall be heirs of salvation, snatches the gold from the crucible, and stores it in God's treasure-house, leaving the dross on earth, and the tempter foiled. That the path of suffering is the one that leads to glory none can doubt, because it is the one the Master trod; but, as, when the night was darkest with Christ, angels came and ministered unto Him, so they come to us; unseen, it may be, by most of God's children, but visible to those to whom is given extended power of sight; and such power comes not by the working of some law, which man, perchance, might call a miracle, but by the operation of the laws already established, as these act upon what is *made ready* to receive its impressions. Just as in the kingdom of Nature there may be two rosebuds on the same stem; the sunlight falls equally on both, and the one opens and blossoms into beauty, while the other, by reason of less vitality, or of some hidden blight, never unfolds its petals at all. When men cavil at and argue about *miracles*, they forget that words are coined by men; and words in many instances may be called necessary evils; though we cannot do without them. They are often quite inadequate to convey the full meaning, or even a partially correct idea, of what is in the mind of a speaker, unless the person who is addressed is like-minded. Words are constantly misunderstood, and none more persistently than the word 'miracle,' which simply means something wonderful, and beyond explanation on ordinary human lines. Miracle is the best word at man's command for embodying in a concise form the expansive and illimitable force of God's laws, whenever He sees well to give visible signs of the subtlety and inconceivable power of His will working by law.

Those who open their eyes to the light when it shines upon them, who do not close their eyes to the innumerable proofs in the visible universe of the infinitely greater unseen creation of which Holy Scripture tells us, see in the God-man that centre of power and unity, which makes the visible and the invisible one continuous act of Divine power; and to them the miracles of our Lord in healing the sick are but proofs of His perfect knowledge of what, in each case, was needed, and of His almighty power to apply the remedy. He who did such mighty works has told His servants to 'work while it is day;' that is, to do their duty in that state of life in which they are placed, and by so doing prepare themselves for that higher life which is to come. Countless as are the members of the human family, so are the kinds of sacrifice which God requires of them; for every sacrifice must be the expression of the individual, and no two persons are precisely alike in thought or feeling. That which would be a great sacrifice to one person, would be no sacrifice to another. It follows, therefore, that man can only judge of the moral influence of the law of sacrifice by observing that certain causes lead to certain results; that high principles and faith in God shape themselves into noble deeds. Father Damien and Chinese Gordon are modern illustrations of self-sacrifice.

Those who in this world find and keep in the narrow path of duty will form the Church of the firstborn, of whom St. John writes, 'I saw thrones, and they'—the blessed ones called unto the marriage supper of the Lamb—'sat upon them, and judgment was given unto them: and I saw the souls of them that were beheaded for the witness of Jesus, and for the Word of God, and which had not worshipped the beast, neither his image, neither had received his mark upon their foreheads, or in their hands; and they lived and reigned with Christ a thousand years. But the rest of the dead lived not again until the thousand years were finished. This is the first resurrection. Blessed and holy is he that hath part in the first resurrection: on such the second death hath no power, but they shall be priests of God and of Christ, and shall reign with Him a thousand years.' 'Write,' said a voice which came out of the throne, saying, 'Praise our God, all ye His servants, and ye that fear Him, both small and great.' 'Write,' said the 'voice' to St. John in Patmos, 'Blessed are they which are called to the marriage supper of the Lamb.' And he who spoke added, 'These are the true sayings of God.' Then, the 'beloved disciple' tells us, 'I fell at His feet to worship Him. And He said unto me, See thou do it not: I am thy fellow-servant, and of thy brethren that have the testimony of Jesus: worship God: for the testimony of Jesus is the spirit of prophecy.' Those inspired words raised the veil which in part prevented even St. John from seeing clearly. The 'voice' came out of the throne, and the holy man thought it was the voice of God, and fell down to worship Him that spake. St. John had not then, in his deep humility, learned how entirely the soul of redeemed man is one with God. His mistake became the occasion for the glorious revelation of the harmony in heaven, which will be so perfect, that the voice of God and man will be as one. Man's nearness to God is proclaimed by the 'voice' proceeding from the throne on which God was seated. Yet the revelation vouchsafed to St. John was but a confirmation of the words which Jesus spoke on earth of His disciples, when He prayed to His Father for them, and not for them alone, but for them also which should believe on Him through their word : ' The glory which Thou gavest me I have given them ; that they may be one, even as we are one : I in them, and Thou in Me, that they may be made perfect in one ; and that the world may know that Thou hast sent Me, and hast loved *them* as Thou hast loved *Me*.' St. Paul, writing ' to the saints and faithful brethren in Christ' at Colosse, says, 'we do not cease to pray for you, and to desire that ye might be filled with the knowledge of His will in all wisdom and spiritual understanding ; that ye might walk worthy of the Lord unto all pleasing, being fruitful in every good work, and increasing in the knowledge of God ; strengthened with all might, according to His glorious power, unto all patience and long-suffering with joyfulness, giving thanks unto the Father, which hath made us meet to be partakers of the inheritance of the saints in light : Who hath delivered us from the power of darkness, and hath translated us into the kingdom of His dear Son.'

In these passages of Holy Scripture, man's character, his greatness, and his destiny, are plainly revealed. With evidences of the antiquity of the Old Testament prophecies, and the proofs of their fulfilment in the New Testament, and in secular history, man is inexcusable if he fails to apprehend that his composite nature is both Divine and human. He *is* what God made him, whether he knows it or not; and he is responsible for not knowing and believing, because he is a free agent. Why, then, does he not 'rise to his birthright,' and maintain his position? Simply because he wills to do what Eve did in the garden of Eden: he listens 'to cunningly devised fables.' The darkness that has been gathering and increasing in volume and density, century after century, around this vital subject seems to be Satan's masterpiece. As long as he can make man forget who and what he is, he knows that his work is comparatively easy; since, apart from God and immortality, there is nothing worth living for. It is a Satanic work to cast the dark pall of unbelief in the supernatural over the mind of man; because, severed from the supernatural, the world itself is but as a kaleidoscope, and man one of its shifting particles. It is only as a great fair, and men and women are the puppets, dancing, singing, or working at some toy, with head or hands, until the time comes when they must go off the stage to make room for others.

Some Christians feel that it is their duty and

privilege to pray for those who, because they do not believe in the 'Hearer and Answerer of Prayer,' cannot pray for themselves. They pray for the living and for the departed, for in so doing they know that they are following the example of their Lord, since prayers for the dead are known to have been a part of the services of the Temple, in which He joined. They believe that 'if there is really any organized connection between the present and the future life, it follows that we who are alive and those who are dead must constitute one organic body, intimately united. This union must be a union not merely in word, but in reality. It must be the same kind of union as that which binds us together in this life with the same obligations and the same privileges. The brotherhood of humanity extends beyond the grave, and is not limited by the accidents of the temporal and corporeal senses.' St. Paul says, 'If so be that we suffer with Him, that we may be also glorified together.' Hence the practical nature of prayer for one another, and the consequent value of it. Human society, whether under its secular or spiritual aspect, being so constituted that each of us has it in his or her power to confer benefits upon others by direct personal action, it follows, as a matter of necessity, that as prayer for ourselves ensures personal blessings, so intercessory prayers are but the complement of our direct activity of service on behalf of a brother. Why then is this intercessory prayer to be cut short at the moment of death, as some believe it is? If our brotherhood lasts beyond the grave, how can we suppose that its spiritual privileges are suddenly annihilated? Christ on His mediatorial throne is ever praying for us. St. John saw 'the four-and-twenty elders fall down before the Lamb, having everyone of them harps, and golden vials full of incense, which is the prayers of saints.' Also, he saw an angel come and stand before God at the altar, 'having a golden censer; and there was given unto him much incense; that he should offer it with the prayers of all saints upon the golden altar which was before the throne. And the smoke of the incense which came with the prayers of the saints, ascended up before God out of the angel's hand.'

Here we are taught that glorified men and angels present the prayers of the saints, the children of Christ's Kingdom, to the Lamb. In Hades the rich man interceded for his brethren with Abraham. Are the members of Christ's body on earth to be the only ones debarred from the inestimable privilege of intercessory prayer for all who need it, wherever they may be? 'The liberal soul shall be made fat; and he that watereth shall be watered also himself.' 'He which soweth sparingly shall reap also sparingly, and he which soweth bountifully shall reap also bountifully.' 'Ask, and it shall be given you; seek and ye shall find; knock and it shall be opened unto you.' 'Pray one for another, that ye may be healed. The effectual fervent prayer of a righteous man availeth much.' These words were spoken by St. James, one of the first Bishops of the Church, who taught that men must be 'doers of the Word, and not hearers only.' Doubtless, the words of his Master, 'Why call ye me Lord, Lord, and do not the things which I say,' were still ringing in his ears, when he wrote his 'General Epistle.' That epistle is a model charge for Bishops of all ages; for it is so fully in touch with the Divine and human parts of man's nature. In this particular St. James is a remarkable anticipation of some of the most successful teachers of men. His were no faltering utterances. Expediency was no part of his creed. Temporizing was no part of his practice. He was far beyond the mere *endurance* of the trials which fall to the lot of all who walk in the way of the Cross when he wrote, ' My brethren, count it all joy when ye fall into divers temptations ; knowing this, that the trying of your faith worketh patience. But let patience have her perfect work, that ye may be perfect and entire, wanting nothing.' His was the faith that could remove mountains ; and of what God had given him he, as a faithful steward, dispensed to others. But lest any should pride themselves upon extraordinary gifts and graces, he warns them, 'Do not err, my beloved brethren. Every good gift and every perfect gift is from above, and cometh down from the Father of lights, with whom is no variableness, neither shadow of turning.' Lest any should be satisfied with the cloak of religion, he writes, 'If any man among you seem to be religious, and bridleth not his tongue, this man's religion is vain. Pure religion and undefiled before God and the Father is this: to visit the fatherless and widows in their affliction, and to keep himself unspotted from the world.' No lesson was ever more needed in the world, in any period of the world's history, than this. St. James tells his readers of the fruits of their fallen human nature; of the hardness and pride of the rich in their dealings with the poor; and then he appeals to their Divine nature. 'Hearken, my beloved brethren, Hath not God chosen the poor of this world, rich in faith, and heirs of that kingdom which He hath promised to them that love Him?' When he has warned man of the just judgment, 'For he shall have judgment without mercy, that hath showed no mercy,' he asks, 'What doth it profit, my brethren, though a man say he hath faith, and have not works? Can faith save him?' St. James answers the question in an eloquent passage on the relation between faith and works. As one reads it in the light of the nineteenth-century teaching that is put forth by some easy-going Christians, who believe that since

Christ has died for them, they have nothing to do for Him or for themselves, the fact that the Holy Scriptures were written for all time, and that holy men of old wrote under the direct influence of the Spirit of Truth, forces itself upon the mind. The power of Truth embodied in the question, 'Wilt thou know, O vain man, that faith without works is dead?' makes itself felt, as the words one by one fall upon the mind, the heart, and the conscience of man, as only absolute truth can. Then St. James deals with that great gift of God to man, the gift of speech, which distinguishes him from all other creatures: and he shows that the organ of speech has, through sin, become 'an unruly evil, full of deadly poison.' Truly, the father of lies has done, and is doing, his work in the world well; for everywhere now falsehood and its attendant evils prevail; even as they did when St. James wrote of the sins of the tongue, and added, in the meek and lowly spirit of his Lord, 'My brethren, these things ought not so to be.' Again, he charges them, 'Submit yourselves therefore to God. Resist the devil, and he will flee from you. Draw nigh to God, and He will draw nigh to you.' He tells them, 'There is one Lawgiver, who is able to save and to destroy,' and warns them of the uncertainty of life. 'Go to now, ye that say, To-day or to-morrow we will go into such a city, and continue there a year, and buy and sell, and get gain:

whereas ye know not what shall be on the morrow. For what is your life? It is even a vapour, that appeareth for a little while, and then vanisheth away.' The practical, searching words, 'To him that knoweth to do good, and doeth it not, to him it is sin,' are followed by his withering condemnation of the rich, who defraud the poor and condemn the just; who heap up treasure, and are wanton. St. James concludes with an exhortation to patience and prayer, and urges his brethren to take 'the prophets, who have spoken in the name of the Lord, for an example of suffering affliction and of patience.'

As there is no such thing as chance in the universe, we look for design in all things, and find it everywhere. In the history of the Kingdom of Christ, there is no more perfect bit of mosaic work to be found than the account of the appointment of the first Bishop of Jerusalem.

1. His name was James, a 'supplanter,' or 'underminer.' The Church was to act like leaven in the world; to undermine and change the existing state of religion and morals; in short, to supplant all other religions as time rolled on, and in the end to reign supreme.

2. The See of the first Bishop was Jerusalem, 'the vision of peace.' The seat of this Bishopric was soon to be destroyed; as if to teach men that the Church was not a temporal, but a spiritual

organization; and that, as she was born from above, and set up on earth as God's witness for the exposition of Truth, her visible aspect must make it impossible for man to believe that her progressive strength, her victorious march through the world, and her ultimate triumph over the powers of darkness, were due merely to the human energy of her members.

3. As Bishop of the Mother of all Churches, St. James presided at the first General Council at Jerusalem; and after St. Peter and others had delivered their addresses, he pronounced judgment. None questioned his authority. He said, '*My sentence is*,' and all present, from the least to the greatest, submitted to his judgment: a simple historical fact, recorded in Holy Scripture, which nullifies the subsequent Petrine claim, that Christ when on earth ordained St. Peter as Head of the visible Church.

The only Head that the Church universal ever has acknowledged, or ever will, is the Lord Jesus Christ. It is the glory of the Church that her Head is in heaven. We do not, when thinking of the Head of the Church, realize as fully as we ought to do that He is a *Man*: as man withdrawn from mortal sight for a time, as God, ever with His Church; thus connecting heaven and earth, thus uniting the Divine and human.

Profound in depth and marvellous in beauty is

the character of St. John the Divine. He is an illustration of those who fulfil their mission in the kingdoms of nature and grace by diligently and silently working out the purpose of their being, as in God's sight. They live under the shadow of the Cross with a halo of light around them; and though storms rage and the troubled waters which dash upon the shore of Time often threaten to overwhelm them, they are kept by the power of God; and those who look through the veil that divides the visible and the invisible can see that the halo of light is caused by a greater Light than the sun of our solar system; for the clouds which darken the natural world cannot intercept it.

The Blessed Virgin Mary, who was pronounced by an archangel to be 'full of grace,' and therefore chosen to be the mother of Jesus, is His mother still; and in accordance with God's law must ever be nearer to her Divine Son than any other human being can be; but next to her seems to be St. John, whose name signifies the grace or gift of God. It is much to be able to touch but the fringe of the garment of him who lay upon the Saviour's breast; for in doing this we know that some virtue will flow into our souls. It is much to get within the outermost circle of the glories which encircle the 'beloved disciple,' for at once we have light enough to discern the greatness of humility, which was so conspicuous a trait in his character. Just as when standing beneath the shadow of a lofty mountain, with nothing but the far-off light of stars to dispel the total darkness, we look up and see in the infinite vastness of the blue vault above us one shining world after another revealing itself to our mortal vision; so as we study the character of St. John we see unfolded the attributes which bring man into closest communion with his Maker, and which enable him to soar on the wings of love from the valley of earth to the heights of heaven, and there see a vision of the glory that shall be hereafter. St. John ever seemed to be nearest to his Divine Master, and he was left on earth longer than either of the other apostles: left, as it would seem, because he was the apostle of love, and because the great God of love would have lingering still on earth, in human form, the highest type of His own immortal love for man. St. John was the only apostle who stood with St. Mary and Mary Magdalene at the foot of the Cross during the three hours' agony; and it is *there* that we must all be in spirit if we would catch glimpses of spiritual realities, and learn to understand in any measure the visions that were vouchsafed to St. John. What a typical group that was on Calvary! The God of the universe, incarnate, sacrificing Himself for mankind, and making propitiation for the sins of the whole world. At the foot of the Cross Purity, Love and Penitence. God and angels looked on from above. The world looked on from beneath, and mocked. The Christ of God looked down from the Altar of Sacrifice on His mother and on the disciple whom He loved, and gave them to each other. As God, Christ loved them both with the Divine love that was fully manifested by the Incarnation. As perfect man He loved His mother with a perfect human love. In one sense she was all that He could call His own in the world that He had created; and as such He gave her to that disciple who remained faithful when all the others had forsaken Him. St. John had the spirit of power and of love; and from the moment when Jesus said to His mother, 'Behold thy Son,' that disciple was to her in name and reality the 'gift of God,' and he took her unto his own home.

Our Lord taught that as 'every good tree bringeth forth good fruit; but a corrupt tree bringeth forth evil fruit,' so it is with man, 'ye shall know them by their fruits.' St. Paul tells us that 'the fruit of the Spirit is love, joy, peace, long-suffering, gentleness, goodness, faith, meekness, temperance.' That none of these fruits were wanting in the home that was provided for the Blessed Virgin on earth until the time should come when she would be again and for ever with her Divine Son we may be well assured; but none may know—for it has not been revealed—how widespread has been the influence of the lives of St. Mary and St. John : none the less real and lasting, spiritually and practically, because they are not recorded. Spiritual things are spiritually discerned, and the Christ-like lives of the Virgin and St. John would not be understood by the world. Nevertheless, all who came within their circle of influence, and gave heed to the teaching of the Holy Spirit, became centres of light and attraction to others ; and the last great day will reveal the number of men and women who through nearly two thousand years have walked in the footprints of the 'Mother of Jesus' and the 'beloved disciple.'

No one can read carefully the Gospel of St. John without being struck with its high spiritual tone. It opens out to our view more of heaven than either of the other Gospels, for Christ's inner life, and His longing for the salvation of man, are written as in letters of light. The great intercessory prayer to His Father lays bare the heart of Jesus, and draws every loving soul nearer to its God. From beginning to end the Gospel of St. John is superhuman. No wonder, then, that those who close their eyes to the light that will alone enable them to see the truth cannot understand it. No wonder that controversy has raged round the sacramental teachings of our Lord as recorded by St. John. The followers of St. John know that his testimony is true, and they bear witness to the truth : they 'love not the world, neither the things that are in the world'; for they know that 'all that is in the world, the lust of the flesh and the lust of the eyes, and the pride of life, is not of the Father, but is of the world. And the world passeth away and the lust thereof; but he that doeth the will of God abideth for ever.'

> 'On champions, blest, in Jesus' name,
>   Short be your strife, your triumph full,
> Till every heart have caught your flame,
>   And, lighten'd of the world's misrule,
> Ye soar those elder saints to meet,
> Gathered long since at Jesus' feet,
> No world of passions to destroy,
> Your prayers and struggles o'er, your task all praise and joy.'*

St. Peter, another of the three most eminent apostles, is an illustration of types of believers who are more visible to the world than the types of St. John. Disciples after St. John's pattern live in shady walks untrodden by men of the world; and their work, like that of the coral-insect, goes on unseen for the most part by the eye of man. The practical character of St. Peter is one which the great mass of mankind can understand better than the mystical character of St. John; therefore, so far as human judgment enables men to form a correct opinion, the followers of St. Peter are likely to far out-number those of St. John. The Founder of the Church, as the Creator and Lawgiver of the

* Keble.

universe, knew precisely how the law of conformity to type would work in the spiritual as in the natural world, and He appointed agents to establish and carry on the work of the new kingdom who should be most precisely fitted for that work in its various forms and relations. None can fail to see how eminently the zeal that was a prominent characteristic of St. Peter qualified him for the work which he had to do. It also served another purpose. It was the means by which he learned his own weakness and imperfection; for it led him into scenes of trial and temptation where his boasted faith and love and courage failed. Christ knew all that it would one day be in the power of His disciple to accomplish by reason of his strong will, and the general force of his character; but he had to be disciplined for his work; he had to learn that his strength was weakness unless it was supported by the Divine power that was in him. Whatever lingering thoughts of self-sufficiency may have been cherished by St. Peter after his many falls must all have vanished when Christ said to him, ' *When thou art converted, strengthen thy brethren.*'

The life of St. Peter shadows forth the history of that part of the Catholic Church which has made St. Peter its patron saint. The same idiosyncracies which distinguished St. Peter are to be found in the Church which is called after his name, and also in the individual members of that Church.

The faith and the love of St. Peter were often manifested, but before his conversion they as often failed. He tried in his own strength to walk upon the sea and failed. He followed our Lord into the hall of judgment and in the moment of temptation failed. The zeal of St. Peter would have led him to make three tabernacles on the Mount of Transfiguration—one for Christ, one for Moses, and one for Elias; but his zeal was not according to knowledge.

When tracing the life of St. Peter and the history of the Roman Church the truth of the old proverb, 'Coming events cast their shadows before,' is borne in upon the mind. The lie in Pilate's judgment-hall is a prefigurement of a long series of lies and forgeries endorsed by Roman authority to prop up the claims of the Papacy to universal dominion. Peter's striking with the sword symbolizes the carnal weapons which Rome used so freely in the Middle Ages; his cursing, Rome's anathemas; his self-confidence, Rome's presumption; his hasty words, which drew upon him the stern rebuke of the Saviour, 'Get thee behind Me, Satan.' prefigures the arrogance of Rome, which has always impeded the work of the Universal Church by making her appear to the world less powerful than she is; because the world sees only her outwardly divided state, caused by the sins of her members, and naturally asks, 'Where is the one Catholic and

Apostolic Church which you Christians profess to believe in?' Her children know. She is where Christ laid the foundation-stones; she is in the world, where she has fought and conquered, and where she fights and conquers now; for the arm of the God of battles is her defence and shield. She must fight to the end, until the Church Militant becomes the Church Triumphant. Meanwhile, she must give heed to the lessons of Holy Scripture, for they 'were written for our learning.'

Not without a sufficient reason did our Lord choose Simon's ship, and sit down in it to teach the people. Past, present, and future are one to Him. The Church of St. Peter, with all its record of faith and works, with its later exclusive pretensions to the authority and infallibility which belong to the Catholic Church in every land; her history as a National Church, her schismatical art in altering the Œcumenical creed of the Church and causing the schism between East and West; the lives of her primates and of her individual members, were all known to the Church's Lord. The use which the Popes of Rome would make of the fact that He sat down and taught the multitude from *Peter's* ship was not hidden from Him who knoweth all things. Nevertheless, from that ship the Lord taught, and 'when He had left speaking,' it was to Simon Peter that the command was given, 'Launch out into the deep, and let down your nets for a draught. And Simon Peter answering him said unto him, Master, we have toiled all the night and have taken nothing; nevertheless, at thy word I will let down the net.' Simon's words were followed by an act of obedience which brought its reward, for 'they inclosed a great multitude of fishes.' Then we are told, 'their net brake.' It brake, although Jesus was in the ship. Man had made the net. And men now use, and in time past have used, various humanly-devised means to catch men, and Peter's net and Peter's ship, which are types of Peter's faith and Church, were no exception to the law of imperfection which rules in all earthly things. Then is given in the inspired record what no member of the Catholic Church should ever forget. When Simon's net brake they beckoned unto their partners which were in the other ship that they should come and help them. And they came.' What was the result? Both ships were filled with the draught of fishes. Success followed the act of obedience to Christ's command combined with *united* action. But what followed? The ships began to sink. The Lord was there, and His servants were acting in unison under His command; but, humanly speaking, the work was too great. As a trial of faith the ships were allowed to begin to sink, and simultaneously the faith of Simon failed, for 'he fell down at Jesus' knees, saying, Depart from me, for I am a sinful man, O Lord.' Here is a clear foreshadowing of the career of the Roman Church. Simon's loss of faith and his words, 'Depart from me,' seem in the clearer light of fulfilled prophecy to anticipate the fear that the Church of St. Peter was in danger when the Isidorean decretals, which elevate the Bishop of Rome to the throne of Christ, were promulgated; and the still existing fear that the old ship may even yet founder; for the decretals, though proved to be forgeries and admitted to be so by Roman authority, are still quoted and used by Rome to uphold the dogma of Papal infallibility. We are not told that the faith of St. James and St. John faltered, but we know that when Simon's faith failed both ships began to sink; and we know also that when corruptions crept into that portion of the Church which was established at Rome, and additions were made to the 'faith once for all delivered to the saints,' other portions of the Church left their first love. To the world the Church may seem to be sinking, but her children have no fear for her. At the moment when the waters of Genesareth seemed about to close over the ships, the words fell from the lips of Jesus, 'Fear not,' and the mountains that surround the lake gave back the sound; and on and on through the centuries those words have been echoed, touching the hearts and reviving the faith of all loyal members of the Church. And now that the shadows of evening seem to be gathering around us, and watchmen are warning the unbelieving world that night is at hand, and that the Judge is at the door, we hear those words again and look up, knowing that our redemption draweth nigh.

Some episodes of St. Peter's life must be classed among the most painful ones of Holy Scripture. They are recorded for the benefit of mankind, and as warnings to those who are of like disposition. The facts of history cannot be blotted out because men refuse to acknowledge them, or remain wilfully ignorant of them; and the greatest admirers of St. Peter after his conversion and repentance, are those who realize the disgrace of his fall, even as he realized it himself. Nothing shows the nobility of his nature more than the fact that the Gospel of St. Mark was written at his dictation. The penitent humility of St. Peter may have been the reason for his suppressing his own name and substituting that of his amanuensis. It was the same spirit which led the great Apostle to direct St. Mark to make precise records of his grievous falls as a warning to future generations.

Regarded from the highest standpoint—which none can doubt was St. Peter's own—his denial of his Lord was a sin of deeper dye than the betrayal of Judas; and it must have touched the human heart of Jesus, and caused a pang that would be felt at its core. We have evidence in ourselves that it was so; for we know that the words 'What thou doest, do quickly,' were spoken by Christ to Judas with calm dignity; for the disciple then lying on Jesus' breast tells us that 'no man at the table knew for what intent He spake this unto him: for some thought, because Judas had the bag, that Jesus had said unto him, Buy those things that we have need of against the feast: or, that he should give something to the poor.' The base denial of even a knowledge of his Lord, following so closely upon Peter's self-glorification—'Although all shall be offended, yet will not I'—was noticed only by a look. 'The Lord turned and looked upon Peter.' It was enough. Divine love touched his higher nature, and 'he went out and wept bitterly.' How well a true heart, though encompassed with the imperfections incident to humanity, can understand this! In comparison with St. Peter, Judas had ever stood afar off, while St. Peter was one of the three most favoured disciples. The denial of Peter was like a wife stabbing her husband; the betrayal of Judas was more like a servant deserting his master, or a subject turning traitor to his king, and for a paltry bribe delivering him into the hands of his enemies. In the one case there was remorse without repentance, and Judas went to his own place by his own hand, and of his own free will, and there he awaits his sentence. In the other case, repentance immediately followed the sin; and that the grace of final perseverance was given to St. Peter we know from his after life and martyrdom. A realization of the depth of his fall can alone enable us to form an adequate conception of the height to which he attained. The power of united repentance and perseverance is nowhere more clearly demonstrated than in the case of St. Peter, unless it be in the case of the woman who came to bathe the feet of Jesus with her tears. She had been a great sinner; but with her whole being she had turned away from sin and clung to the feet of Jesus; and the full repentance and self-sacrifice were rewarded. She loved much, because He who first loved her had forgiven much; and love of God for Himself alone is a certain means of securing God's greatest gifts and highest favours; only, it must never be forgotten that no thought of reward, *as such*, must mingle with that love, or its perfection will be destroyed. Love for Jesus, as her Saviour, was all the woman had in her heart.

'Get thee behind Me, Satan,' was said to St. Peter when he, in his mistaken zeal, would have hindered the work of redemption. 'Touch Me not,' was said to Mary Magdalen, when she would have clung to the feet of the risen Lord; not because He shrank from the touch of mortality, as, but a moment before, He had drawn her towards Him by lovingly breathing forth her name, but to teach her and future ages the lesson, that even love must not interfere with duty, and bind Him to earth, when His work henceforth was to be on His mediatorial throne in heaven. He had already told His disciples, ' Let not your heart be troubled : ye believe in God, believe also in Me. In My Father's house are many mansions : if it were not so I would have told you. I go to prepare a place for you. And if I go and prepare a place for you, I will come again, and receive you unto Myself; that where I am, there ye may be also. I will not leave you comfortless. I will come to you.' ' Hath He said, and shall He not do it?' 'Heaven and earth shall pass away, but My word shall not pass away.' 'Touch Me not,' only meant ' Do not touch me now.' In every Eucharist those who draw near to partake of the living Bread which came down from heaven, touch the risen Christ, in accordance with His own command, ' Take, eat ; This is My body: This is My blood.' ' He that eateth My flesh, and drinketh My blood, dwelleth in Me, and I in him.'

The Church is passing through a fiery trial in this latter end of the nineteenth century. The world is bringing forth all her old weapons, and forging new ones, wherewith to attack her. Unbelief, in its most deadly forms, is gaining strength. Indifference is degenerating into contempt ; and mere professors are persecuting the living members of the Church. But the Lord says, ' Fear not '; 'no weapon formed against thee shall prosper; My kindness shall not depart from thee, neither shall the covenant of My peace be removed.' Now, as of old, God is in His holy temple. He comes to His Altar-throne, and gives Himself to all who will receive Him. But when He, the Prince of Peace, and lover of concord, comes to His Church, what does He find? Alas! He finds discord where all should be harmony; estrangement where all should be brotherly love; controversy where all should be of one mind. He hears the members of His Church profess their creed; He sees them bringing the little children to Him through the waters of Baptism, but He hears one say, 'I am of the Greek Church'; and another, 'I am of the Roman Church'; and a third, 'I am of the Anglican Church'; just as in earlier days some said, 'I am of Paul; and I of Apollos; and I of Cephas.' 'Is Christ divided?' Surely not. He Himself has said, 'I am the Vine, ye are the branches'; and the Father of Glory gave His Son to be the 'Head over all things to the Church, which is His body.' As the Catholic Church is then *one* in Christ, the members should confront the world as one mighty army, fighting against the evil that is in the world, instead of exhausting their strength and wasting their precious time in warring against each other. In the kingdom of nature every tree has its own

THE GREAT KINGDOM

special characteristic ; its mode of growth, its leaves, its blossoms, and its fruits. By these each tree is known from all others. There may be, nay, there are, varieties of the same tree or plant, but the essential character is plainly discernible in each variety, so that the species is at once recognised. It, ideally, is the same in Christ's Kingdom, and as when we see an acorn we know that it grew upon an oak, so when we see men who can prove their claim to be successors of the Apostles, holding the faith of the Apostles, teaching the Word of God in its entirety, and dispensing the Sacraments in accordance with primitive usage and the law of the Church, we know that they are members of the body of Christ, treading in the footprints of the apostles, and obeying the command of their Lord, ' Feed My sheep.'

For those who follow the Good Shepherd there is prepared an 'inheritance incorruptible and undefiled, and that fadeth not away.' By Baptism they are made members of the 'One Holy, Catholic, and Apostolic Church,' wherever they dwell throughout the whole world. They are the stones which St. Peter tells us are 'built up a spiritual house, an holy priesthood, to offer up spiritual sacrifices acceptable to God by Jesus Christ.' Their Lord has promised to give to him that overcometh ' a white stone, and in the stone a new name written, which no man knoweth saving he that receiveth it': a name that shall never be blotted out of the book of the everlasting Kingdom of the Lord Jesus Christ, who is the 'King of kings and Lord of lords.'

THE END.

www.ingramcontent.com/pod-product-compliance
Lightning Source LLC
Chambersburg PA
CBHW032145230426
43672CB00011B/2453